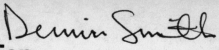

Softcops & Fen

Softcops, inspired by Michel Foucault's *Discipline and Punish*, was first staged by the Royal Shakespeare Company in 1984. It explores the theme of law and order and examines the way that social institutions lead us to conform through discipline and punishment to accepted patterns of behaviour.

'*Softcops* is Foucault rendered as a music-hall turn and a Victorian freak show, with music by Brecht and Gilbert and Sullivan . . . After all the tedious Anglo-Saxon academic renderings of Foucault, Churchill's vision is pure fresh air. One wishes the master and his acolytes had her gift for the drama of ideas . . . I can remember few evenings when theatre and history combined to give such intelligent fun.'
Michael Ignatieff, *Times Literary Supplement*

Fen, winner of the Susan Smith Blackburn Prize, was first staged by the Joint Stock Theatre Group in 1983.

'Influenced by Mary Chamberlain's *Fen Women*, and lovingly researched by Joint Stock, it scrutinises the lives of the low paid women potato pickers of the fen: people trapped by a life that is dour, sombre and flat as the land they inhabit.' Ros Asquith, *City Limits*

'The playwright pins down her poetic subject matter in dialogue of impressive vigour and economy.' Michael Coveney, *Financial Times*

Caryl Churchill has written for the stage, television and radio. Her stage plays include *Owners* (Royal Court Theatre Upstairs, 1972), *Objections to Sex and Violence* (Royal Court, 1975), *Light Shining in Buckinghamshire* (for Joint Stock, Theatre Upstairs, 1976), *Vinegar Tom* (for Monstrous Regiment, Half Moon and ICA, London, and on tour, 1976), *Traps* (Theatre Upstairs, 1977), *Cloud Nine* (Joint Stock at the Royal Court and on tour, 1979; De Lys Theatre, New York, 1981), *Three More Sleepless Nights* (Soho Poly and Theatre Upstairs, 1980), *Top Girls* (Royal Court, London and Joseph Papp's Public Theatre, New York, 1982), *Fen* (Joint Stock), Almeida Theatre and Royal Court, London, and on tour, and Public Theatre, New York, 1983; winner of the 1983 Susan Smith Blackburn Prize), *Softcops* (RSC at the Pit, 1984), *A Mouthful of Birds* (with David Lan, for Joint Stock at the Royal Court and on tour, 1986), *Serious Money* (Royal Court, Wyndham's Theatre, London and Joseph Papp's Public Theatre, New York, 1987), *Ice Cream* (Royal Court, 1989), *Mad Forest* (Royal Court, 1990), *Lives of the Great Poisoners* (Arnolfini, Bristol, 1991) and *The Skriker* (Royal National Theatre, 1994).

by the same author

CHURCHILL PLAYS: ONE
    Owners, Vinegar Tom, Traps, Light Shining in
    Buckinghamshire, Cloud Nine

CHURCHILL PLAYS: TWO
    Softcops, Top Girls, Fen, Serious Money

SERIOUS MONEY

TOP GIRLS
    (also published in the Methuen Student Edition with
    commentary and notes)

ICE CREAM

MAD FOREST

LIVES OF THE GREAT POISONERS
    (with Orlando Gough and Ian Spink)

THE SKRIKER

CARYL CHURCHILL

Softcops
& Fen

Methuen Drama

Methuen Modern Plays

This two-play volume first published in 1986 by Methuen London Ltd
Copyright © 1986 by Caryl Churchill
Reprinted 1990, 1992
Reissued with a new cover design 1994
by Methuen Drama
an imprint of Reed Consumer Books Ltd
Michelin House, 81 Fulham Road, London SW3 6RB
and Auckland, Melbourne, Singapore and Toronto
and distributed in the United States of America
by Heinemann, a division of Reed Publishing (USA) Inc.
361 Hanover Street, Portsmouth, New Hampshire NH 03801 3959

Softcops first published as a Methuen Paperback original in 1984 by
Methuen London and Methuen Inc.
Copyright © 1983, 1986 by Caryl Churchill

Fen first published as a Methuen Paperback original in 1984 by Methuen
London Ltd, in association with Joint Stock Theatre Group,
123 Tottenham Court Road, London W1P 9HN
Copyright © 1983, 1986 by Caryl Churchill
Girls' Song copyright © 1983, 1986 by Ilona Sekacz

Set in IBM 10pt Journal by Ⱥ Tek-Art, Croydon, Surrey
Printed and bound in Great Britain by
Cox & Wyman Ltd, Reading, Berkshire

British Library Cataloguing in Publication Data

Churchill, Caryl
Softcops; & Fen.
I. Title   II. Churchill, Caryl. Fen
822'.914   PR6053.H785

ISBN 0-413-41200-8

The front cover photograph is by Lesley McIntyre and shows
Linda Bassett from *Fen*.

In *Softcops* Caryl Churchill has reflected some ideas from *Surveiller at
Punir* by Michel Foucault, published by Gallimard, Paris, for which she is
most grateful.

In *Fen*, 'Girls' Song' is based on quotations from *Fen Women* by Mary
Chamberlain (Virago, 1977). The pitchfork murder story in Scene Ten is
based on material in an unpublished work by Charles Hansford.

Softcops

Softcops was first presented by the Royal Shakespeare Company at the Barbican Pit on 2nd January 1984, with the following cast:

DUVAL	Christopher Bowen
MINISTER	John Carlisle
VIDOCQ	Geoffrey Freshwater
ELOQUENT RICH MAN	Hepburn Graham
LAFAYETTE	Tom Mannion
MAGISTRATE BENTHAM CONSPIRATOR	} Pip Miller
SCHOOLBOY OLDER BROTHER WARDER	} David Shaw-Parker
BOY	Brian Parr
HEADMASTER HOLIDAYMAKER	} Bill Stewart
LACENAIRE CONSPIRATOR	} Malcolm Storry
PIERRE	Ian Talbot
MAN ON RACK WARDER	} Philip Walsh

Other parts: WORKERS, SCHOOL CHILDREN, RICH MEN, CHAIN GANG etc., played by members of the cast.
The Medici String Quartet: Paul Robertson *violin*, David Matthews *violin*, Ivo van der Werff *viola*, Anthony Lewis *cello*

Directed by Howard Davies
Designed by Bob Crowley
Music by Nigel Hess
Lighting by Michael Colf
Movement by Stuart Hopps
Sound by John A. Leonard
Stage Manager Michael Dembowicz
Deputy Stage Manager Jill Macfarlane
Assistant Stage Manager Stephen Dobbin

The play takes place in Paris in the nineteenth century, mainly in the 1830s.

Author's Note

Vidocq and Lacenaire are the original cop and robber, Vidocq, the criminal who became chief of police using the same skills of disguise and cunning, and Lacenaire, the glamorous and ineffectual murderer and petty thief, who was briefly a romantic hero. They both wrote their memoirs, and from the London Library you can take home the original edition of Vidocq's, each volume signed firmly with his name.

I read them after reading Michel Foucault's *Discipline and Punish*, which fascinatingly analyses the change in methods of control and punishment from tearing the victim apart with horses to simply watching him. Jeremy Bentham comes in here, the inventor of the panopticon, the tower from which one person can watch and control many, an idea that goes right through the way society is organised.

I had had an idea for a play called *Softcops*, which was to be about the soft methods of control, schools, hospitals, social workers, when I came across the Foucault book, and was so thrilled with it that I set the play not here and now but in nineteenth century France, where Vidocq puts on half a dozen disguises and Lacenaire is feted by the rich in his cell, while the king's assassin is quietly disposed of. There is a constant attempt by governments to depoliticise illegal acts, to make criminals a separate class from the rest of society so that subversion will not be general, and part of this process is the invention of the detective and the criminal, the cop and the robber.

Caryl Churchill (First published in *RSC News*, Winter 1983)

Further note

Softcops was originally written in 1978, under a Labour Government, when the question of soft controls seemed more relevant than in 1984, the year of its first production, when Thatcher was dismantling the welfare state. That year, audiences were particularly alive to the connection between Bentham's panopticon and Orwell's Big Brother. In 1985, as this edition goes to press, the Government are attempting to depoliticise the miners and the rioters by emphasising a 'criminal element'.

Caryl Churchill *1985*

Production note

The production was developed by the director, designer, composer, choreographer, actors, musicians and myself in a way that I have not attempted to describe — I have for instance kept the original stage direction I wrote for the rescue of Lafayette from the scaffold rather than try to convey the choreography by which it was done. Nor have I stipulated that the set is a neglected room in a great house, that the actors are in evening dress, or that there is a string quartet on stage throughout. These things come from Howard Davies' production and it does not seem right to appropriate them as part of the play.

Caryl Churchill 1985

A high scaffold is being erected. PIERRE *is anxiously supervising and helping drape it in black cloth and put up posters and placards. A crocodile of young* BOYS *in uniform crosses the stage with their* HEADMASTER, *circles and stops in front of the scaffold.*

PIERRE. Ah, you've brought them for me. I need children with their soft minds to take the impression. More folds this side. Yes, the minister will see them learning. More, more, it hardly reaches the ground. Not long now. It's worth waiting for.

HEADMASTER. They can stand as long as necessary. They have stood three hours.

PIERRE. I can't hold the nail steady. Thank you. My hands are shaking. I want it to be perfect.

HEADMASTER. While you're waiting, examine your consciences.

PEOPLE *go by, stop, go on, come back, gather some distance from the scaffold. The* CHILDREN *stand motionless.*

PIERRE. I hope the rain keeps off. The dye isn't fast.

HEADMASTER. The design is excellent.

PIERRE. There is a balance if I can get it. Terror, but also information. Information, but also terror. But I dream of something covering several acres and completely transforming — as you know. I won't bore you. But if the minister is impressed today I hope for a park.

HEADMASTER. I'm sure it strikes terror.

CHILDREN. Yes, sir.

HEADMASTER. And makes us love our duty.

CHILDREN. Yes, sir.

HEADMASTER. It's a better lesson than talk. Saves the throat.

PIERRE. Help them with the balance. The event will be horrible but the moral is there. Learn while you're young to worship Reason. Reason is my goddess. Fall at her feet. Unfortunately the minister has happy memories of sheer horror. That sign is crooked. Would it be better lower down? Can the children read it?

The HEADMASTER *indicates a* CHILD, *who reads.*

CHILD. 'Jean Lafayette murdered his employer by strangling and will himself be strangled by hanging by the neck.'

PIERRE. Good, leave it there. Where are the red ribbons? Look, children, red is a symbol of blood and passion, the blood shed by passion and the blood shed by Reason in justice and grief. Grief is symbolised of course by the black.

The WORKMEN *are putting red ribbons on the scaffold.*

Or does it look more striking without the ribbons? Should grief be the dominant theme? Blood can be represented by itself. The procession comes down the hill so the crowd can watch its approach. Doleful music specially composed. I've written a speech for the magistrate and one for each of the condemned men. There are three, I hope you can stay. No, take the ribbons off.

The WORKMEN *start taking the ribbons off.*

When the minister sees the children it will help him grasp the educational —

Music: wind and drums.

They're coming. They're early. Get the ribbons off. Stand back.

The WORKMEN *go. One ribbon is left on.* PIERRE *is watching the procession approach.*

See, see the effect. Where's the minister? We can't start. It's fine in the sunlight, the pigeons fly up. The minister is missing the procession.

The procession comes in: the MAGISTRATE *in black; the*
EXECUTIONER *in red; the* MUSICIANS *and* GUARDS *in*
black and red; black-draped cart; the PRISONER *in the cart in*
black except for his right hand in a red glove which he holds
up. A placard round his neck: Jacques Duval, thief.

PIERRE (*to the* MAGISTRATE). Welcome, welcome, sir. It's
very good of you to take part in this experimental — Excuse
me, there's something wrong here. We have the wrong placard
I think. (*He takes down the notice about Lafayette and hunts*
for one about Duval.) Thief, thief, leg of lamb. (*To*
MAGISTRATE:) I hope the walk hasn't tired you, sir. Slight
problem, nothing to worry about, I'm afraid the minister has
been detained. It's not quite time, I think. I wonder if you
could just go round again. You could wait here, sir, if you'd
rather and the rest of the procession could just go round the
square. No need to go back up the hill. That's right, people
will move aside, music again too, it's very moving, well done,
music, music.

The procession slowly circles. PIERRE *puts up the correct*
notice.

HEADMASTER. That gentleman is the magistrate. See his wise
face, kind and stern. Here comes the cart, see the villain. You
can see the weakness and evil. His right hand which did the evil
deed is clad in red. One of these men is the executioner — ah,
that one in red. He carries an instrument of justice. What does
red symbolise?

CHILD. Blood, sir.

HEADMASTER. And?

CHILD. Passion, sir.

PIERRE. Get that ribbon off, off.

PIERRE *realises the* WORKMEN *have gone and gets the*
ribbon off himself.

HEADMASTER. What will he do with the wicked man?

CHILD. Hang him, sir.

HEADMASTER. Wrong.

CHILD. Hurt him, sir.

HEADMASTER. Hurt him, yes, can somebody be more precise?

CHILD. Cut his hand off, sir.

HEADMASTER. Yes, you can see it written on the notice. He will cut off the hand that stole the leg of lamb.

CHILD. Please, sir, shouldn't they cut his leg off, sir?

Meanwhile the MINISTER *has arrived and is greeted by* PIERRE.

PIERRE. They came down the hill, a moment of great solemnity, the power of the law struck home to the heart and mind, the pigeons flew up. You see the notices, sir, explaining, so everyone understands what is happening and isn't carried away by emotion.

MINISTER. They can't read.

PIERRE. The magistrate also makes a speech, sir. And each condemned man makes a speech. Some of them can read, sir. A few of them. Maybe not.

HEADMASTER. Your country loves its children like a father. And when the children are bad the country grieves like a father. And punishes like a father.

The procession stops by the scaffold.

MAGISTRATE. There's a word here not very clearly written.

PIERRE. I can't read my own writing. Whatever you think.

MAGISTRATE. Execution?

PIERRE. Very likely. (*To* MINISTER:) A headmaster has brought his pupils. The use of punishment as education —

MAGISTRATE. 'This is a day of mourning.'

PIERRE. Ah, ah, excuse me, execration.

MAGISTRATE. 'Day of mourning.'

PIERRE. No, the word, here, execration.

MAGISTRATE. Very good, I would never have thought of that. Execration. Let me make a note. 'This is a day of mourning.

We are, you see, in black. We mourn that one of our citizens has broken the law. We mourn that we must separate ourselves from this citizen and inflict this penalty upon him. Black symbolises our grief and our — ha — execration of his crime. This man has with his right hand —'

PIERRE. Hold it up, hold it up.

MAGISTRATE. — 'committed an act against his fellow men. And it is with grief that his right hand will be taken from him. We do not rejoice in vengeance. There will be no singing and dancing, no cursing and fighting. It is a sad necessity for him and for us. Our social order —'

Meanwhile one of the CHILDREN *fidgets, is taken out of line by the* HEADMASTER, *caned on the hand and returned to his place. The rest of the* CHILDREN *stand motionless.*

MINISTER. Can't we get on with the punishment?

PIERRE. This is the general introduction to the whole —

MINISTER. Never bore a mob.

PIERRE. We're about half-way.

MINISTER. Where's the executioner?

PIERRE (*to* MAGISTRATE). Thank you, we'll stop there, thank you.

PIERRE claps; HEADMASTER *joins in;* CHILDREN *join in. By then* PIERRE *has stopped.*

Now the condemned man will speak. Listen and learn. Music.

Music. The prisoner, DUVAL, *climbs on to the scaffold. Cheers and jeers from the* CROWD.

Wait till the music stops. Now.

DUVAL. I, Jacques Duval.

PIERRE. Go on.

DUVAL. I, Jacques Duval.

PIERRE. Don't cry, speak up. (*To the* MINISTER:) Tears of repentance.

DUVAL. I, Jacques Duval. Under sentence of having my right hand cut off —

PIERRE. Hold it up. Good.

DUVAL. Call out. Call out . . .

PIERRE. Theft, crime of theft, cut off for the crime —

DUVAL. Theft, crime of theft, cut off. Fellow citizens. Call out to my fellow citizens.

PIERRE. Learn —

DUVAL. Learn by my terrible example. Never steal even if you're hungry because . . .

PIERRE. Because it is against the laws —

DUVAL. Laws of our beloved country. And your hand will be cut off.

PIERRE. Up, up, that's right.

DUVAL. I'm very sorry what I done.

PIERRE. Good.

DUVAL. And submit, is it? Submit the punishment the judge give me. Gladly. Gladly submit. Judge give me. And . . .

PIERRE. I am happy —

DUVAL. — I am happy —

PIERRE. — to be an example —

DUVAL. — example

PIERRE. — to you all.

DUVAL. — all.

PIERRE. Watch —

DUVAL. Watch what is done to me today and remember it tomorrow.

PIERRE. If you are sorry for me —

DUVAL. Yes, that's it.

PIERRE. Keep the law. Go on.

DUVAL. Go on.

PIERRE. No, keep the law.

DUVAL. Yes.

PIERRE. And then I'll know my pain did some good.

DUVAL. I don't know what comes after.

PIERRE. That's all.

MINISTER. Where's the executioner?

HEADMASTER. Are all your eyes open?

MAN IN CROWD. Jacques! I'm here. Jacques!

DUVAL. Don't look!

> DUVAL's *hand is cut off and displayed to the* CROWD *by the* EXECUTIONER. *He faints and is put in the cart.* PIERRE *indicates to the* MUSICIANS *that they should play. The* GUARDS *take the cart out,* DUVAL's FRIEND *running after. The* MUSICIANS *play. One of the children,* LUC, *turns aside to be sick. The others stand motionless.*

MINISTER. It's over very quickly. I don't count the talking. When I was a boy one punishment would last from noon till sunset. You could buy food and drink. I remember one time they lit a fire to throw the corpse on in the late afternoon and he held on and held on and they had to build the fire up again in the evening. It was still glowing at midnight, and people still standing. That was the wheel, of course, you don't see it now. People don't want to read, they don't want speeches. You'll drive them away, and what's the use of a punishment if nobody sees it? What brings a crowd, it's very simple, is agony, I'm not saying they don't appreciate something fine. They like an executioner who's good at his job. They like fine instruments. Nothing upsets a crowd more than hacking. But they like something unusual and they like a man to stay conscious so he doesn't miss it.

PIERRE. There's a good crowd here today.

MINISTER. That's the novelty. They don't want a school, they want a festival.

PIERRE. A festival means riots. People attack the executioner.

MINISTER. And the soldiers shoot them down.

The HEADMASTER *has got the sick child,* LUC, *and made him stand with his arms over his head.*

HEADMASTER. Now control yourself. Stand with your arms up till I tell you.

MINISTER. Listen, my boy. People have vile dreams. The man who dares cut a throat while he's awake is their hero. But then justice dares cut and burn and tear that man's body, far beyond what he did and beyond their dreams. So they worship us. That's why it's a festival.

PIERRE. But I don't want them to be caught up. Their hearts may beat a little faster but all the time they must be thinking.

The music starts again for the approach of the procession — the return of the GUARDS *and the cart.*

MINISTER. While the fire burned and long after it died down there was considerable fornication. Not only among the poor.

PIERRE. Ah look, sir, excuse me, down the hill.

MINISTER. I found my way to a lady who had never been more than civil to me and my hand under her skirt found her ready for hours of ingenuity beyond my dreams. Next day she received me for tea as usual. The people went about their work quite silently.

PIERRE. I want them to look at the illegal act in the perspective of the operation of society and the light of Reason.

The cart comes in with LAFAYETTE, *a murderer. He is already speaking in the cart and continues when he is transferred to the scaffold.* PIERRE *suddenly remembers that the placard must be changed and hurries to do it.*

LAFAYETTE. Lafayette. Look at me. Remember the name. Lafayette. Murderer. Murderer. Want to know what I did? Killed my boss. Killed old daddy Anatole right in his office. He was shouting like he does, know how he shouts. And I was on him, hands round his neck, would he stop shouting, would he hell. So I kept hanging on, didn't I. I'm meant to say sorry for that. Sorry sorry sorry sorry sorry. Do you think I am? I shit on the judges. I shit on my boss. I shit on you. I really did shit on my boss. Do you shit on your boss? You didn't kill him though, did you, I'm the killer. And I'm the one going to die. Want to die instead? You can if you like. I don't want to. You do it. You kill him instead, all right? He goes a horrible colour, wait and see. I'm not sorry, I'm glad. It wasn't easy but I did it. Lafayette did it.

Meanwhile:

PIERRE. This isn't what we arranged he would say.

MINISTER. Just hang him.

PIERRE. I wrote a speech.

MINISTER. Where's the executioner?

PIERRE (*to* LAFAYETTE). Look, you agreed what you were going to say.

LAFAYETTE *strikes him. Instant brawl.* LAFAYETTE *is seized by the* EXECUTIONER *and* GUARDS, *a hood put over his head and a noose round his neck. The* CROWD *throws stones, shouts, climbs on to the scaffold. The* CHILDREN *scatter.* LAFAYETTE *is hoisted up. The* EXECUTIONER *is hit by a stone. The* MINISTER *and* MAGISTRATE *escape from the scaffold.* PIERRE *tries to defend the scaffold and is knocked down, pulling the black cloth with him. The rope hanging* LAFAYETTE *is cut by one of the* CROWD. *He gets down and tries to run but is pulled down by someone else. The scaffold is broken. The* CROWD *has formed into two groups, one beats up* LAFAYETTE *and one beats up the* EXECUTIONER. *The* DIGNITARIES *and* MUSICIANS *are standing aside in a huddle. The* CHILDREN *are watching what is done to* LAFAYETTE *and the* EXECUTIONER. *A line of* SOLDIERS *comes on with fixed bayonets and advances. The* CROWD *scatters and disappears.* LAFAYETTE *and the* EXECUTIONER *are lying on the ground.* LAFAYETTE *sits up, still with the hood and noose on, and collapses again. One of the* MUSICIANS *blows a few wild notes, a* DRUMMER *joins in. One of the* SOLDIERS *turns towards them. Silence.*

The SOLDIERS *go. The* MAGISTRATE *and* MINISTER *go.*
The CHILDREN *get back into a crocodile and* LUC *lifts his*
arms again. PIERRE *gets out from under the black cloth,*
blood on his face. The GUARDS *and* MUSICIANS *put the*
pieces of broken scaffold in the cart, put LAFAYETTE *and*
the EXECUTIONER *on top, and go out. Just* PIERRE *and the*
HEADMASTER *and the* CHILDREN *are left.*

What I visualise you see. Is a Garden of Laws. Where, over
several acres, with flowering bushes, families would stroll on
a Sunday. And there would be displayed every kind of crime
and punishment. Different coloured hats. Different coloured
posters. Guides to give lectures on civic duty and moral
feeling. And people would walk gravely and soberly and
reflect. And for the worst crime. Parricide. An iron cage
hanging high up in the sky. Symbolic of the rejection by
heaven and earth. From anywhere in the city you could look
up. And see him hanging there, in the sun, in the snow. Year
after year. Quietly take it to heart. A daily lesson.

The HEADMASTER *wipes blood off* PIERRE's *face.*

HEADMASTER (*to* LUC). You may put your arms down now.

The HEADMASTER *and* CHILDREN *go out.* PIERRE *is left*
alone. The MINISTER *and* VIDOCQ *approach from opposite*
sides.

MINISTER. The best informer we have is Vidocq. He's a villain
but he catches villains. I've a good mind to persuade him to
change his way of life and make him Chief of Police.

VIDOCQ. Here comes the minister. He can't do without me. But
everyone treats informers like dirt. I've a good mind to
persuade him to trust me and make me Chief of Police.

MINISTER. Is that you, Vidocq?

VIDOCQ. What is the real colour of Vidocq's hair? I don't know
myself. Grey by now. Do I really wear spectacles? Is this
moustache real or stuck on? If it's real, did I grow it as a
disguise? Or will it be a disguise when I shave it off? Who have
you come to see, sir? And do you see him?

MINISTER. I see someone useful.

VIDOCQ. Always that, sir. I'm twenty men and all of them at your service.

MINISTER. I have a special job for you, Vidocq.

VIDOCQ. I'll be glad to do it, sir, whatever it is.

MINISTER (*aside*). This is going too fast. He'll never accept if I ask him point blank.

VIDOCQ (*aside*). I'm being too eager. He won't believe I'm not tricking him.

MINISTER. We'll talk about it later. You may not be the right person for this particular enterprise.

VIDOCQ. Yes, I'm not that interested in sneaking.

MINISTER. I can manage without your services.

VIDOCQ. I can do without you an all.

MINISTER (*aside*). This is terrible.

VIDOCQ (*aside*). This is terrible. Sir, I hear you've had a great success in arresting the notorious regicide, Fieschi.

MINISTER. It's not generally known but I don't mind telling you. He was discovered yesterday drunk in an attic.

VIDOCQ. The police don't often have such luck.

MINISTER. It takes skill to catch a man like that.

VIDOCQ. Yes, I'm quite surprised they managed it.

MINISTER. The police force is a force to be reckoned with.

VIDOCQ. I've nothing against the police force as such.

MINISTER. It's not as efficient as it might be.

VIDOCQ. That's exactly what I think myself.

MINISTER. Ah.

PIERRE *approaches*.

PIERRE. Excuse me, sir, did you say Fieschi? Fieschi who tried to murder the king with an infernal machine? That will count as regicide, sir, parricide, even though the king wasn't hurt. Might it not be the occasion, sir, for the use of the iron cage I mentioned to you which would hang above the Garden of Laws and —

MINISTER. Aren't you ashamed?

PIERRE. It didn't go quite according to plan, sir.

MINISTER. I should have told the soldiers to shoot.

PIERRE. Next time —

MINISTER. Next time I will have the prisoners flogged. And ten men taken from the crowd.

PIERRE. If the prepared speeches —

MINISTER. They will all be gagged.

PIERRE. My idea, sir, is that in the park —

MINISTER. Never. Tell him, Vidocq. You were a boy when pain was seen to be necessary. We are dealing with a wild animal and we keep it off us with raw meat and whips. We don't teach it to sit up and beg and feed it sugar lumps. It bit you this morning and I'm glad.

PIERRE. Reason is my goddess.

MINISTER. Reason uses whips. The minister has no further use for your services.

PIERRE. Thank you, sir.

PIERRE *starts to leave.*

MINISTER. I'd have Fieschi ten days dying but that has all been abolished. But you and I, Vidocq, know what it is to live in fear.

VIDOCQ. Come back here. Not a rich man?

PIERRE. No.

VIDOCQ. Poor but honest?

PIERRE. And not stupid.

VIDOCQ. Idealist? Visionary? Reformer?

PIERRE. It will happen. If not me, someone else.

VIDOCQ. No, never someone else. Me. Me. If you think of a good idea get the credit. My slightest whim I go for like a life's ambition. Here's some money for you.

VIDOCQ *throws a gold coin on the ground.*

All you've got to do is pick it up. But if you don't do it before I count a hundred, I'll shoot you in the leg. I count in ones. The gun is loaded. The coin is real gold. It's not tied to a string. Well?

PIERRE *looks from one to the other and laughs nervously.*

Neither of us will touch you. You have a hundred seconds to pick up the coin. But of course you might get cramp and fall down. There might be an earthquake. Someone else might run up and get the coin first. And then I will shoot you in the leg. Never mind what I'm after.

PIERRE. All right.

VIDOCQ *starts to count.* PIERRE *stands still till ten then walks very slowly and picks up the coin.*

VIDOCQ. Again?

PIERRE. Wouldn't mind.

VIDOCQ. No, this time we're going to do it different. Come here. Hands behind your back. You can have another coin just for asking. But if you do I'll hit you in the face.

PIERRE. No you won't.

VIDOCQ. It's not so bad as being shot in the leg. Want a coin?

PIERRE. No.

VIDOCQ. Real gold.

PIERRE. No.

VIDOCQ. Off you go then. There you are. It's not what the punishment is, sir, it's knowing you're going to get it. You could take a whole year to kill a man and nobody cares because nobody expects to get caught. You can cover the whole town with posters and nobody reads them because nobody expects to get caught. I've never been caught.

PIERRE. I never thought of that.

MINISTER. It's not true. Vidocq has convictions for theft, blackmail —

VIDOCQ. But I never did any of that. It was always a mistake. I happened to look like the man that done it. I was walking past at the time. Somebody had it in for me. I have done some jobs, I will admit, but you couldn't tell me one of them.

MINISTER. You're saying the police make mistakes?

VIDOCQ. Say you divided the country into ten areas, then into ten divisions, ten subdivisions, ten branches, ten sections, where are we getting, ten policemen in each section.

MINISTER. A million policemen?

VIDOCQ. It's not the number so much as the shape. And at the top a strong man.

MINISTER. A strong man at the top.

VIDOCQ. Do you know what a card index is, sir?

MINISTER. Little boxes.

VIDOCQ. With cards in them, with names on, in the order of the alphabet.

MINISTER. A friend of mine is a naturalist and I believe he —

VIDOCQ. You want a box with all the criminals. And another box with all the kinds of crime. You get a blackmail, b, look it up, who's done blackmail before, Vidocq, V. look him up, how he operates, where you find him, you've got me.

MINISTER. You don't want me to get you.

VIDOCQ. No, sir, if you took my advice I'd have to change my way of life.

MINISTER (*aside*). He said he'd have to change his way of life.

VIDOCQ (*aside*). Dare I suggest it now?

MINISTER (*aside*). Is this the moment to make the offer?

VIDOCQ. Of course I am a professional where crime is concerned. I couldn't lead a life completely cut off from it.

MINISTER (*aside*). Is he saying he won't go straight?

I have known you a long time and I know what you are.

VIDOCQ (*aside*). Is he saying he can't ever trust me?

PIERRE. I've had an idea. I think Monsieur Vidocq would make an excellent Chief of Police. I know you both think my ideas never work out.

MINISTER. But you know Monsieur Vidocq would never want to be a policeman.

VIDOCQ. You know the minister would never trust me.

PIERRE. The card index box appeals to Reason.

VIDOCQ. The boy's not stupid, you know.

MINISTER. Not at all. He's one of the brightest in my department.

VIDOCQ. You should listen to what he says.

MINISTER. I value his opinion very highly. I didn't really dismiss him just now.

VIDOCQ *gives* PIERRE *a gold coin.*

VIDOCQ. You can think of this coin as the perfect crime, no trouble, from the days before Vidocq was Chief of Police.

PIERRE (*to the* MINISTER). Sir, about the park —

MINISTER. Chief of Police.

The MINISTER *and* VIDOCQ *embrace.*

Crimes against property is an area of concern. I have land. I have warehouses. In the bad old days the peasants used to take liberties, chop down trees for firewood, that sort of thing, perfectly understandable, the old feudal landlords were monsters. But you can't have that now the land's owned by respectable citizens. You can't have that in warehouses. I lose thousands.

VIDOCQ. Wherever you get a lot of workers, sir, you'll get a lot of bad characters.

MINISTER. I sometimes think you see that if I took one of them as an example and set up a wheel by the factory gate —

VIDOCQ. Not a wheel, sir, a card index box. We'll have the bad characters in a box. You'll see. You can trust the rest. And the police will live so close to that criminal class, take informers from it, know it like itself, so every time someone reaches for a gold coin, wham, he's hit in the face.

MINISTER. I regret the disappearance of the thumbscrew. But that's the nostalgia of an old man.

PIERRE. A golden age. Crime will be eliminated.

VIDOCQ. Not entirely eliminated, no. It is my profession.

MINISTER. Vidocq, can I trust you?

VIDOCQ. I'm going to be famous.

PIERRE *takes out a book and reads.*

PIERRE. The memoirs of Vidocq.

VIDOCQ. Every night a new crime against property. I want to catch the gang redhanded. I get drinking with their leader. I seem to be from the provinces. I seem not to want him to guess I've escaped from prison. I seem to let him get me drunk.

ANTIN *and* VIDOCQ 2, *who looks nothing like* VIDOCQ.

ANTIN. Stick with me and you'll be all right. I'll settle Vidocq one of these days.

VIDOCQ 2. Everyone says that.

ANTIN. Right then, we'll settle him tonight.

VIDOCQ 2. You know where he lives?

ANTIN. Coming?

VIDOCQ. So we wait for me outside my door. But I don't show up all night.

ANTIN. I'll get him tomorrow. Now then, you interested in a job?

VIDOCQ. So we plan a robbery for the next night. And to his surprise the police turn up.

ANTIN. Here, what's this?

VIDOCQ 2. I'm Vidocq.

Tableau of VIDOCQ 2 *arresting* ANTIN.

PIERRE (*reads*). A butcher was robbed and murdered on the road.

VIDOCQ. I get two of them Court and Raoul. The third's a retired customs officer. I go to his village. He's mending a road with thirty other men. If I try to arrest him, they'll kill me.

VIDOCQ 3, *quite different again, and* PONS GERARD, VIDOCQ *embraces* PONS.

VIDOCQ 3. How's the family?

PONS. What? what?

VIDOCQ 3. Have I changed so much?

PONS. I can't quite —

VIDOCQ 3 (*whispers*). Friend of Court and Raoul.

PONS (*for the benefit of the other men*). Ah ah, my dear old friend.

VIDOCQ. So I get him alone.

PONS. Who was it got them?

VIDOCQ 3. Who do you think?

PONS. I'd like to see that Vidocq. What I'd do to him.

PONS *gives* VIDOCQ *a drink.*

VIDOCQ 3. What you'd do to Vidocq is give him a drink.

PONS. Don't make me laugh.

VIDOCQ 3. I'm Vidocq.

Tableau — VIDOCQ 3 *arrests* PONS GERARD.

PIERRE (*reads*). There was cholera in Paris. Three hundred people died every day. Riots broke out. The army was having trouble. It was thought Louis-Philippe might lose his throne.

VIDOCQ. There's a group building a barricade so I go up behind them with a few men in plain clothes. I'm carrying a red flag, which makes it easier to get about. They're looking in front where the soldiers are coming. I take hold of their leader, Colombat. I say, Come along now, I'm Vidocq.

What VIDOCQ *describes is happening.* VIDOCQ 4 *with a red flag arrests* COLOMBAT.

VIDOCQ 4. Come along now, I'm Vidocq.

Tableau — VIDOCQ 4 *arrests* COLOMBAT.

VIDOCQ. We cleared five barricades so the army had freedom of movement. The revolt was suppressed. It was a matter of public order. More than half the people on the street were villains. I've welcomed every kind of government, always hoping for order. Better my way than the army shooting. Which they still did of course. One young man couldn't get the bloodshed out of his mind and subsequently tried to kill the king. I disguised myself as a duchess one day and shook the king's hand.

PIERRE. Speaking of killing the king, sir, the regicide, the one with the infernal machine, sir, I was wondering if we could make a display —

VIDOCQ. Make a display? of a regicide?

MINISTER. The rack? — no.

PIERRE. The iron cage — everyone stares up — amazing spectacle —

VIDOCQ. A regicide? You want to take people's attention off. You don't want to make an example of a regicide, people follow an example. What you want for a spectacle is someone good-looking and a bit out of the ordinary. Lacenaire.

MINISTER. Who's Lacenaire?

VIDOCQ. Second-rate little villain. Bungles half his jobs.

MINISTER. Then what's the point?

PIERRE. I've heard of Lacenaire.

VIDOCQ. He's writing his memoirs. People pass them round on little bits of paper.

PIERRE. That could be a wonderful means of education if he was warning young people against — is he? I suppose not.

VIDOCQ. He's pretty. He writes verses. He'll do.

LACENAIRE *is brought on between two* POLICEMEN.

LACENAIRE (*recites*).
   What is life? What is death? What is virtue? What is
      philosophy?
   Science? Honour? Gold? Friendship's not much either.
   If there's a God, he only loves himself.
   Why are you frightened of death? Ah, nothingness.
   Curse me — I laugh. Curse me — I'm firm in my frenzy.
   But if I'd believed in goodness I would have been good.

VIDOCQ. Perfect.

LACENAIRE. I didn't commit murder for money, I did it for
blood. I decided to become the scourge of society. Father said
I would end on the guillotine.

MINISTER. Isn't this dangerous?

VIDOCQ. Marvellous, isn't it, and he's not even good at his job.
His famous robberies only got him a few hundred. He makes a
noise, he trips over, he faints. He quarrels with all his friends,
he betrays them, he blackmails, he gets blackmailed. He
doesn't plan. Or he makes plans and tells everyone what he's
going to do so it's all over Paris before he's done it. The other
villains despise him. He's a complete failure.

LACENAIRE. I can't live out there. I'd rather be in prison with
my brothers. There's a society of the rich and a society of the
wretched. I identify with the wretched. I too have been
rejected. I too seek vengeance. Murder is an example to others.
I am an example, a man of good birth, a poetic genius, who
has deliberately made himself a murderer. With these hands.

RICH MEN *are arriving for a feast in* LACENAIRE's *cell. They
cheer and clap as* LACENAIRE *talks.* LACENAIRE *is sat
down, his face wiped, hair combed, drink poured for him,
food put before him. The* MINISTER, VIDOCQ, PIERRE *and
the* HEADMASTER *are all there. A* PHRENOLOGIST *feels*
LACENAIRE's *head and a* WRITER *takes down every word
he says.*

RICH MEN. He's so young.
   All he's been through.

Yes but you can see in his eyes.
Never trust eyes like that.
It's the shape of his skull.
No, it's his free will.
His pure self-interest.
I conduct my business like that.

MINISTER. He looks like a success.

VIDOCQ. Do you trust me?

MINISTER. I think I have to.

LACENAIRE. My mother never loved me. That may be the
explanation you're looking for. If I'd been born forty years
earlier I would have been a hero of the revolution. I would like
to pull the city down.

RICH MAN. I pulled down six of my houses yesterday and the
tenants ran out like rats.

LACENAIRE. I'll save a fine chair, a painting of Napoleon and a
silk scarf, and the rest can go. I don't like ugliness.

ANOTHER RICH MAN. Nor do I, have nothing in my house but
beautiful things.

LACENAIRE. I hate beauty worse.

Applause.

PHRENOLOGIST. The bumps on his head indicate that he is not
aggressive. He is rather of a timid disposition.

LACENAIRE. Timid? Timid? With this hand — Yes, of course, go
on. Write down every word I say. Feel my bumps. Cut me up
when I'm dead. It's still not me. You'll never know. I am a
secret.

WRITER. What? What?

ANOTHER RICH MAN. 'You'll never know. I am a secret.'

PIERRE. But he shouldn't be a secret if he's a spectacle.

HEADMASTER. My pupils have no time for secrets.

PIERRE. If Lacenaire had been properly educated he'd feel the
right things for people to see. There's something new here, I

can't quite —

LACENAIRE. Why do you kill animals?

ANOTHER RICH MAN. Me? I don't think —

LACENAIRE. Don't you eat meat? Don't you hunt? You have designed ways of torturing animals as delicate as your furnishings. And you call me a murderer.

ANOTHER RICH MAN (*to* PIERRE). He killed his kitten by hitting it against the wall and he cried for hours.

LACENAIRE. I have a horror of all suffering. But you only understand if it happens to someone like you. So you murder every day. I have sacrificed myself to prove it. You can't understand love, but you understand fear. I'm going to die tomorrow. And when I die, everything I've ever seen will come to an end. The city will fall. Your chandeliers are down. That's my vengeance.

ANOTHER RICH MAN. Wear this for me tomorrow.

ANOTHER RICH MAN. Wear this for me.

LACENAIRE *spits at him. Laughter and clapping.*

LACENAIRE. I won't wear your jewels because you'll take them off my corpse and say 'Lacenaire wore this for me'. And the glory of my death is not yours.

MINISTER. Half an hour on the rack and he wouldn't talk so much.

VIDOCQ. He couldn't be better if I'd invented him. Lacenaire, do you know who I am?

LACENAIRE. A fat idiot like the rest.

VIDOCQ. Vidocq, Chief of Police.

LACENAIRE. A fat idiot worse than the rest.

Laughter and clapping.

PIERRE. I think you er believe in Reason?

LACENAIRE. I believe in necessity.

PIERRE. Ah. I believe in Reason. I don't think either of us believes in God.

LACENAIRE. Don't try to make friends with me.

PIERRE. No, of course. Sorry.

LACENAIRE. No, I don't believe in God. I tried for a moment yesterday afternoon. My only virtue is sensibility. No one has ever had such a prodigious facility for writing verse. Good verse. And bad verse.

RICH MEN. Recite a poem.
Sing a song.
Oh please.

LACENAIRE. I never like showing my compositions.

RICH MEN. Yes yes.

LACENAIRE. *The Thief Asks the King for a Job.*

RICH MEN. This song is banned.
Oh wonderful.

LACENAIRE *stands and sings.*

LACENAIRE. I'm such a thief your Majesty,
I'm such a villain you'll agree
I'd make a great policeman.

I spend cash that's not my own,
Never hear the victim groan —
I'd make a great minister.

I'm cunning, greedy, really bad,
A lot of people think I'm mad —
I'd make a great king.

Laughter, applause, cheers.

I could just as well have written the opposite. I happened to meet some republicans in prison one day, that's all. We've never had liberty yet, not for one day. Is it worth all the blood? And you tell me to respect human life. I'm committing suicide, that's all. A very spectacular suicide with a very big knife. Does anyone dare say I'm not committing suicide?

RICH MEN *sing in imitation of* LACENAIRE.

RICH MEN. What a brilliant demonstration,
Symbol of his generation —
You'll make a great martyr.

All your friends will thrill to see you,
How we wish that we could be you —

LACENAIRE. Friends? What friends? My friends don't like me. I
am their leader to overthrow the world and they won't see it.
They're jealous. I miss them.

RICH MEN. They're just villains and they hate you,
Only we appreciate you —
Murder is Art!

Further shouts from the RICH MEN.

The metaphysics!
Lacenaire, I share your soul!

LACENAIRE. They are gods. And you are little lice on their
bodies. Pop. Little specks of blood.

RICH MAN. Lacenaire, I can imagine you robbing me. I'd wake
up in the night. Is someone there? I get out of bed my heart
beating. Was it a cat? Someone is breathing. I stop breathing.
Yes, someone is breathing. I strike a light. It's knocked out of
my hand. My arm is forced up behind my back. I'm tied to a
chair. My eyes are getting used to the dark. I see you moving
about my room. You throw my clothes on the floor. You find
my jewels and fill your pockets. You slash the mattress and
find the gold. You pull down the velvet curtains and throw
them over my head and force them into my mouth, the chair
falls over, I'm suffocating inside the curtains. You kick free of
them, you're leaving. Lacenaire! You pity me. You pull the
curtains off. You pick the chair up and me on it. Oh Lacenaire.
You slap my face. The taste of blood in my mouth. You put
your knife deep into my chest. Lacenaire, Lacenaire. Let me
give you this ring. Put it on your finger. Ah. You would ruin
me if you were free.

LACENAIRE *is by now quite passive, lets the ring be put on
his finger.*

RICH MEN. Lacenaire, you would kill me.
You would rape my wife on the table.
You would rape me.
You would rape the little schoolchildren.
You would burn my house, I would run through the hall with my hair on fire screaming Lacenaire, Lacenaire.

They are all giving him jewellery and money, embracing him, snatching off his shoe as a souvenior. One of them pulls down his own trousers.

Stand on me, Lacenaire, stand on me. On me, on me. Stand on me, I'm so rich. Stand on me, Lacenaire, I'm so boring.

Two of them with their trousers down bend over and the others help LACENAIRE up. Others take their trousers down or dance on the table, pour drinks on their heads, rub cake in each other's faces. LACENAIRE stands unsteadily, balanced on two bottoms.

VIDOCQ. You are the greatest living criminal. And in me you have met your match because I am the greatest living detective. I hear you have written your memoirs. After your death I will have them published.

Cheers.

LACENAIRE. No one else could have caught me, so he's got to be a genius. I'll drink to you, Vidocq.

VIDOCQ. Your health, Lacenaire.

Shouts of 'Vidocq', 'Lacenaire'. VIDOCQ is in London with his exhibition: large Dutch painting of a battle, quantity of wax fruit, reaping hook, chopper, thumbscrews etc, manacles and chains, weighted boots, braces, a pen, a black box. VIDOCQ speaks in a French accent as he is speaking English to the public.

VIDOCQ. Ladies and gentlemen, here for the first time in London you can see the great exhibition of the great Vidocq, for many years chief of the sureté in Paris, that is the detective force. I have here many marvels for you and also I will astound you by my skill at disguises which made me able to catch so

many criminals of Paris. First we have here many paintings,
very fine, by Dutch masters, Langendyk, Van der Veldes, and
other works of the Italian, Dutch, Flemish and French schools.
While you are looking excuse me one moment.

He goes out and simultaneously appears, a different VIDOCQ,
from the other side, acknowledging applause.

Thank you, thank you. This is how I catch them you see. The
next exhibit is a collection perfectly unique of tropical fruits,
modelled from wax by a special process now lost so it can
never be repeated. See the pineapple, mango, pomegranite,
guava, in their natural colours, excuse me —

And as before he instantly reappears, transformed.

Thank you. Very kind. Now here we have many souvenirs of
the dark side of Paris life. This reaping hook was an instrument
by which a young man killed his mother. This chopper also has
been soaked in blood. Here is some very old thing, the
thumbscrew, from times not long ago, but also very long ago I
am glad to say. Also these chains, chains of the chain gang, of
prisoners going to the galleys. Now ladies and gentlemen,
regard. These manacles and boots with heavy weights I myself,
Vidocq, wore these in my youth. Yes I myself, Vidocq, was
led astray and falsely accused when a young man, I had some
of the wild spirits of the young, and in spite of these very
heavy chains I escaped, as I tell in my memoirs which are on
sale here today. I escape and offer my services to my country
to work here for the police. Now excuse me while you
examine these things.

He reappears as before.

And now ladies and gentlemen we come to the most exciting
souvenirs of the exhibition. What have we here? We have the
braces, yes the braces that held up the trousers of — Fieschi!
the notorious cowardly regicide, who made an attempt on the
life of King Louis Philippe with an infernal machine. And here
we have a pen. Just a pen? What a pen! It is the pen with
which in his prison cell, under sentence of death for a foul
murder, that most celebrated criminal Lacenaire, the
poet-murderer Lacenaire, wrote his memoirs. With this very

pen. And now ladies and gentlemen, I beg you not to tell anyone when you leave this place what I am going to show you now. Yes, it would bring more people here. But it would spoil the surprise for them. Surprise? No, the shock. Tell your friends there is something very special, very horrible, very unique, they must come themselves to see what it is. Ladies and gentlemen —

VIDOCQ *opens the black box and takes from it a black velvet cushion with an embalmed hand on it.*

— the hand that held the pen. The hand that held the knife. The hand of Lacenaire! The hand of a man put to death on the guillotine of France! The hand of glory! Thank you, thank you.

PIERRE. Lacenaire should have been in the centre of the garden. And overhead in a cage I would have put Fieschi, who tried to kill His Majesty. It would have had such educational value. And now everyone's in the street watching Lacenaire, not knowing what to think of him because nobody's telling them, all dancing and screaming, complete confusion. What I love in people is their reason, but they will leap about. I've decided to be a teacher. I despair of my Garden of Laws. It will never happen. I see it so clearly but I'll never walk down those paths and see among the flowers all those little theatres of punishment. I must give it up.

HEADMASTER. You'll make an excellent teacher.

PIERRE. Vidocq is bringing some order into crime. He knows who the criminals are and he will catch them. But then what? What do you do with them? If you don't use their bodies to demonstrate the power of the law — Never mind. Let someone else solve it. Show me your class.

The HEADMASTER *rings a bell.* SCHOOLCHILDREN *run to their benches. Some of them are wearing harnesses to correct their posture.*

HEADMASTER. Enter

CHILDREN *put one leg over bench.*

your benches.

CHILDREN *put second leg over and sit down.*

Take

CHILDREN *put one hand to their slates.*

your slates.

CHILDREN *take the slates.*

The HEADMASTER *has a wooden clapper with which he signals instructions to the* CHILDREN. *He gives a book to a* CHILD, *signals once, and the* CHILD *starts to read in Latin. The* CHILD *makes a mistake, the* HEADMASTER *signals twice. The* CHILD *goes back, makes the same mistake, the* HEADMASTER *signals twice. The* CHILD *goes back, makes the same mistake, the* HEADMASTER *signals three times. The* CHILD *goes back to the beginning of the passage. Soon the* HEADMASTER *signals for the* CHILD *to stop, one signal. He makes a gesture and signals once. The* CHILDREN *start writing.*

HEADMASTER. The very good, the good, the mediocre, the bad. Four classes. Different badges of different colours. A completely separate group, the shameful, who can join the others when they deserve to. Children can be promoted or demoted so all are under equal pressure to behave well. Everyone has a place on the benches according to how they are classified.

The HEADMASTER *moves among the* CHILDREN, *correcting their positions while they write.*

The body turned slightly to the left. The left foot slightly forward of the right. The distance of the right arm from the body should be two fingers. The thumb should be parallel to the table. The forefinger —

Distant outcry of CROWD.

LUC. Lacenaire!

The CHILDREN *all stop writing. The* HEADMASTER *looks at* LUC. LUC *steps out of his place. The* HEADMASTER *signals once. The* CHILDREN *write.*

PIERRE. Lacenaire should have been in my garden. And Fieschi, who was put to death yesterday before dawn, nobody even came, what a waste. You have heard of him? He —

HEADMASTER. Ugly little fellow like hundreds of others, suddenly gets it into his head to kill the king. Shameful behaviour. Better not to think about it and it disappears. But Lacenaire carries himself well, he has a gift. Not a great poet, but a definite gift. I write occasional hexameters myself. We don't want to do what he did, of course, but boys have a hero for a day. But it doesn't mean you can shout out in class.

The HEADMASTER *canes* LUC *on the hand.* LUC *goes back to his place.*

I rarely have to raise my voice. I rarely have to speak. Two fingers remember. Don't let the forefinger slip down the page.

PIERRE. I see now. They've kept Fieschi a secret because he's dangerous and made a circus out of Lacenaire. Things are changing and I'm not part of them. There must be a new idea I haven't thought of.

The HEADMASTER *corrects the* CHILDREN *while they write.* PIERRE *also walks up and down among the* CHILDREN. *He stops by one in harness.*

PIERRE. Is this a punishment?

HEADMASTER. Good heavens no, it helps his back grow straight. And this boy, you see, was inclined to poke his chin. They will all be normal in time.

PIERRE. Yes of course. I saw it in my garden. It helps the boy. I must learn to be a teacher.

HEADMASTER. You have to know what you want from them every moment of the day.

The distant cry again. LUC *jerks but controls himself. Everyone stops writing for a split second then continues.*

I use the cane very rarely now I have perfected the timetable.

I enjoy my work. I see the results of it. Their bodies can be helped by harnesses. And their minds are fastened every moment of the day to a fine rigid frame.

PIERRE. Thank you, but I can't work in a school. I must go and see what's happening. If I could fasten the prisoner to a frame. Without over-exciting the public. If I could fasten the public to a frame. I think I'm on the brink —

Several PRISONERS *stand together with iron collars round their necks, joined by a chain to a central chain. The last prisoner, a* BOY, *is dragged screaming by a* WARDER *to where another* WARDER *is waiting with a hammer and anvil to put on his collar.* PIERRE *watches with interest.*

BOY. No no no. I'd rather die. Do anything with me but don't put me in the chain gang.

PIERRE. You'd rather die? That's very interesting. Could you tell me why?

BOY. Sir, kind sir, help me, I'm innocent. Don't let them put me in the chain gang. I never done it. No no no.

PIERRE. Does death seem more glorious?

WARDER. Excuse me, sir, we have got a job to do here.

PIERRE. Of course, I'm sorry, don't let me get in the way.

BOY. No no no! Not the chain! No!

PIERRE. Is it the degradation? Are you upset by the prospect of being a spectacle? You will cross the whole country with people jeering at you, is that the problem?

2ND WARDER. Get the bastard over here, will you.

He comes to help.

PIERRE. I understand there is considerable sexual abuse of younger prisoners. Is that something that disgusts you? Would solitary confinement —

BOY. Not the chain, help, I never done it, no. I don't want to go in the chain gang. No no no no no no no.

The BOY *is firmly seized and held down.*

WARDER. Lowest of the low, sir, that's what it is. You can't get no lower than the chain gang.

2ND WARDER. If you don't keep still I might miss.

BOY. No no no.

2ND WARDER. Now.

> BOY *is suddenly absolutely silent and still.* 2ND WARDER *bangs the collar shut.* BOY *gets up and totters to the others.*

WARDER. There you are, lads. That's the lot.

PIERRE. So would you say this is the worst punishment we have in terms of deterrent effect on the prisoners and also on the public who see them pass? Who wouldn't weep to see them. The man will put back his master's hen, the child will put back the biscuit. The crowd gazes in silent awe. They turn back thankful to their honest toil. So would you agree their journey across France is a national education? And could be reinforced with placards and lectures? Perhaps I should travel with the chain gang and give a seminar in every village.

> *A sudden outburst. The* WARDERS *are leaving and the* CHAIN GANG *are alone, they embrace, cheer, laugh, stamp, swear. The* BOY *laughs and cheers loudest of all.*

BOY. Free free free.

PIERRE. I beg your pardon.

WARDER. Not what I'd call an education, sir. I should stand further over here if I was you. No, it teaches bad men how to be worse and it teaches them pride in it.

PIERRE. But what does it teach the crowd who sees them?

WARDER. Teaches the crowd to riot.

PIERRE. Oh dear.

WARDER. Teaches hate of the rich. Scorn of the obedient. Defiance of fate.

PIERRE. Oh but surely —

WARDER. Whole country's in an uproar, sir, when the chain gang's gone through.

PIERRE. That's because there are no placards.

WARDER. Lowest of the low, the chain. Don't have to behave.

Not like you and me with jobs to lose.

PIERRE. You don't envy them, surely?

WARDER. Want to try it, sir? You might enjoy it. I've got a spare
collar here.

'PIERRE. Well, no, ha ha.

WARDER. I shouldn't stand there, sir, if I was you.

The CHAIN GANG *have taken from their pockets ribbons,
plaited straws and flowers, and are decorating themselves and
each other.* PIERRE *approaches them.*

PIERRE. Excuse me. Now you have your chains on, are they very
heavy?

BOY. Out of my way, shitface.

PIERRE. Do you feel your guilt brought home to you? No of
course, you're the poor wretch who's innocent.

BOY. Course I'm not fucking innocent. What you take me for? I
done a murder they never found out. I done two. I done six. I
done a landlord! I done a banker! I done a policeman!

Cheers from the CHAIN GANG. *They start to stamp, dance
and sing. The* WARDERS *go.*

WARDER. I shouldn't stay here, sir, if I was you.

The CHAIN GANG *stamp and dance round singing to the tune
of 'The Marseillaise'.*

CHAIN GANG. What do these people want with us,
Do they think they'll see us cry?
We rejoice in what is done to us
And our judges will die.

PIERRE *hesitates, then approaches them again.*

PIERRE. Supposing I was to write a placard, would you wear it
round your neck?

*He is caught in the circle, tripped and dragged, disappearing
among them as they rush on, singing.*

CHAIN GANG. Pleasure has betrayed you,
She loves us instead.

She'd rather dance along the street
Than die with you in bed.
Pleasure is in chains,
She loves to share our pains,
She follows where the song goes,
Chains chains chains.

Your scorn, your hate, your fear,
All belongs to us.
Your gold you hold so dear
All belongs to us.
We've bought it with our lives,
We'll give it to your wives
    for a kiss
    for a fuck.
When we're free when we're free
Who would you rather be
    you or us?
    Try your luck.
    You or us.
    Try your luck.

Far from home, far from home,
Sometimes we moan and groan and moan.
Look in our eyes, what a surprise,
The black judge dies when he sees our eyes.

Children bear your chains,
They're beating on a drum,
They're blowing on a trumpet
When they see us come.

Children bear your chains,
It's not for very long.
The king and queen will carry them
When they hear our song.

Children break your chains,
They're beating on a drum.
Our star is shining in the sky
And our day will come.

Children break your chains
Beating on a drum
Children break their laws
Our day will come.

Children break your chains
Children break your chains
Children break your chains

The CHAIN GANG *rush off.* PIERRE *is left, battered.*

An OLD MAN *approaches. It is* JEREMY BENTHAM.

BENTHAM. You seem to be suffering, my boy.

PIERRE. Never mind, sir, it's only me. Greatest happiness of the greatest number, sir.

BENTHAM. That's all right then.

PIERRE. Mr Bentham, I know you have advocated solemn executions with black clothing and religious music, and that is why I presume to intrude on your time. I have a small demonstration.

BENTHAM. The death penalty should be abolished.

PIERRE. There's no question of death here. It would take place in a garden. An English garden would be ideal, with roses.

BENTHAM. Roses last from early summer right into the winter. They provide a considerable pleasure of long duration. An act of sexual intercourse is a hundred times more intense a pleasure than the smell of a rose. But the roses last many hundred times longer. So multiplying the degree of pleasure by the duration, the ratio of the pleasure of roses to that of sex is approximately 500 to 1, a comfort to us in our old age.

PIERRE *meanwhile wheels on a stand covered with a black curtain.*

PIERRE. Sir, I too would like to live according to reason and mathematics. If you could support my scheme my garden might become a reality. May I show you?

PIERRE *pulls aside the black curtain. Inside there is a* MAN *on the rack. Posters.*

BENTHAM. I hope this has not been arranged for me.

PIERRE. There's little to see in France now except the chain gang and that seems to cause riots. I've had to accept that what my garden lacks is the ancient extreme punishments. Here you have the shock and at the same time the reasonable explanation of how the crime came about and how to resist any such tendencies in one's own life.

BENTHAM. But this sight is not giving us a pleasure greater than the man's suffering. I've seen enough. Release the man at once.

PIERRE. I must devise punishments that will continue to be a novelty and a real attraction to the public.

BENTHAM. Stop stop. It goes on and on.

PIERRE. That's the perfection. It can go on all day and every day. Don't worry, Mr Bentham, come closer. He doesn't feel a thing. Can you see now? The wheels turn but he is not stretched. It's an optical illusion.

BENTHAM. He's not suffering?

PIERRE. That's my new discovery. There's no need for him to suffer. What matters is that he's seen to suffer. That's what will deter people from crime.

BENTHAM (*to the* MAN *on the rack*). Are you all right?

MAN. I wouldn't mind a cup of tea.

PIERRE. You can get down now, thank you.

PIERRE *gives the* MAN *some money and he goes.*

BENTHAM. Well I'm most relieved. You must want your garden very much. I spent years on a scheme of my own. Talking to architects, looking at land. I spent thousands of pounds of my own money. My brother thought of it first in Russia to supervise the workers in the dockyards. It's an iron cage, glazed, a glass lantern —

PIERRE. An iron cage?

BENTHAM. A central tower. The workers are not naturally obedient or industrious. But they became so.

PIERRE. The workers gaze up at the iron cage?

BENTHAM. No no, your idea has to be reversed. Let me show you. Imagine for once that you're the prisoner. This is your cell, you can't leave it. This is the central tower and I'm the guard. I'll watch whatever you do day and night.

PIERRE. I just have to sit here?

BENTHAM. Of course in Russia they were doing work.

BENTHAM *goes behind the curtain, which is the central tower.* PIERRE *goes on sitting. Time goes by. He fidgets.*

PIERRE. Mr Bentham?

Am I doing it properly?

Do you want me to draw some conclusions? It's not comfortable being watched when you can't see the person watching you. You can see all of us prisoners and we can't see each other. We can't communicate by tapping on the walls because you're watching us. Is that right? Mr Bentham? I understand how it works. Can I get up now?

BENTHAM *comes out of the back of the stand unseen by* PIERRE. *He creeps round so that he's behind him while he talks.* BENTHAM *giggles silently.*

The prisoners can't get strength from each other, is that what you want me to observe?

The darkness of a dungeon is some protection, to be always in the light is pitiless.

I begin to feel you must know what I'm like. I find it quite hard to sit still, I'm energetic by nature, I feel quite nervous.

You get to know each prisoner and you can compare him with the others. But I don't know how the others are behaving. You know everything that's going on and I don't know at all.

I think it's most ingenious, Mr Bentham, an excellent means of control. Without chains, without pain. Can I get up now?

Really, Mr Bentham, I think I have appreciated your idea. Am I supposed to sit here all afternoon?

I'm getting a little bored. I must admit I'd wander off and look at the roses if you weren't keeping an eye on me because I really think I've got everything out of this I can and it's wasting my time to keep me sitting here. Instead of thousands of people watching one prisoner, one person can watch thousands of prisoners. I've always wanted to affect the spectators. You're affecting the person who is seen. This is a complete reversal for me. I think I've learnt everything, Mr Bentham. Is there anything else?

BENTHAM. That you don't need to be watched all the time. What matters is that you think you're watched. The guards can come and go. It is, like your display, an optical illusion.

BENTHAM *goes.*

PIERRE. It's hard to give up my garden. I do have a weakness for a spectacle. But this way is far more reasonable. It's nothing like a theatre. More like a machine. It's a form of power like the steam engine. I just have to apply it.

BOYS *in bleached uniforms walk in in single file and line up silently. A* NEW BOY *arrives.* PIERRE *and the* MINISTER *look on.*

MINISTER. Where are the placards?

PIERRE. Here we have a model reformatory, sir, modern educational methods, the application of Mr Bentham's panopticon —

MINISTER. Don't you hang notices round their necks?

PIERRE. No sir, it's an entirely new —

MINISTER. I was beginning to like the placards.

PIERRE. No sir, you'll find this —

MINISTER. Well I hope they don't knock you down. There's always flogging.

An OLDER BOY *brings the* BOY *to* PIERRE.

PIERRE. You have been sent here because you don't sleep at home.

BOY. I stay awake.

PIERRE. You're a vagabond.

BOY. You're not.

PIERRE. What's your station in life?

BOY. I'm an army officer, forty-two years old.

PIERRE. You're not more than fourteen.

BOY. Write it down.

PIERRE. You will work here. A reformatory is not a prison. There are workshops and there are fields. You have no father?

BOY. My father's got no son.

PIERRE. Nor mother either?

BOY. I'm a miracle.

PIERRE. Here you will live in a group called a family. The other boys are your brothers. Each family has a head, whom you will obey, and is divided into two sections, each with a second in command. You will have a number. You will answer to it at roll call three times a day. Your number is 321. This is your elder brother. He will stay with you all the time. And I will pay constant attention to your case.

MINISTER. Not one of you will be torn apart by horses. And I hope you're grateful. (*To* PIERRE:) You may be on to something this time, my boy. Congratulations.

The MINISTER *and* PIERRE *go off.*

BOY. Do they beat you?

BROTHER. Not any more. If you do wrong they put you in a cell by yourself. And on the wall there's big black letters, God Sees You.

BOY. That's all right. I don't believe in God.

BROTHER. You will though.

BOY. Don't mind what they do if they don't beat me.

BROTHER. We preferred the beatings. But the cell is better for us.

BOY. What sort of thing gets you into trouble?

BROTHER. Speaking when you shouldn't. Walking out of step. Looking up when you should look down.

BOY. But what about stealing? And swearing? And hitting someone in the stomach? And setting fire?

BROTHER. There's no time.

BOY. I do what I like.

BROTHER. But we like to do what we ought.

BOY. I don't.

The line walks round once in single file. The BOY at the back steps backward leaving a space. The BROTHER puts the BOY in the space.

BROTHER. This is your place. We're going to the courtyard now and the monitor inspects our clothes. Then we go to where we sleep. At the first drumroll you get undressed and stand by your hammock. At the second drumroll all the boys on the left on a count of one two three get into their hammocks and lie down. It's quite easy. Then the boys on the right do it. Then we go to sleep. You go to sleep lying on your back with your hands outside the cover. You always go to sleep straight away because you've been working hard all day and then there's military exercise and gymnastics. We'll teach you. You can't talk now.

The BROTHER takes his place at the head of the line.

BOY. What if you stay awake?

BROTHER. You don't.

BOY. What if you do?

BROTHER. If you stay awake, don't open your eyes.

The line starts to walk off. The BOY steps out of his place and watches them. They stop, still leaving his space. They turn and look at him. Suddenly he runs and gets into place, gets into step as they go out.

The stage is empty. Two CONSPIRATORS enter.

CONSPIRATOR A. There's one way that can't fail.

CONSPIRATOR B. What's that?

CONSPIRATOR A. Throw myself under the horses' hooves with the bomb. Either it explodes straight off, or anyway the horses shy and there's a delay and at that moment you go into action with the second bomb, so either way the whole thing goes up.

CONSPIRATOR B. Either way you go up.

CONSPIRATOR A. It can't fail.

CONSPIRATOR B. You'd go that far?

CONSPIRATOR A. Wouldn't you?

CONSPIRATOR B. We can't afford to lose you. Too many of us are dead already.

CONSPIRATOR A. Someone's betraying us, that's why.

CONSPIRATOR B. Yes, someone's playing a double game.

CONSPIRATOR A. It's hard to think one of your friends is a spy.

CONSPIRATOR B. It's impossible. Everyone would give his life.

CONSPIRATOR A. So everyone's equally under suspicion.

CONSPIRATOR B. Even me. Even you.

CONSPIRATOR A. Do you ever feel you can't go on?

CONSPIRATOR B. You stop sleeping.

CONSPIRATOR A. My stomach's water, my eyes itch. I'll be glad when it's over.

CONSPIRATOR B. When you throw the bomb?

CONSPIRATOR A. That or . . .

CONSPIRATOR B. What? What?

CONSPIRATOR A. I sometimes think there's more spies than conspirators. Who plans the assassinations, us or them? Do we only murder so they can arrest us?

CONSPIRATOR B. Listen, listen, what you've always said. However far control goes, subversion —

CONSPIRATOR A. We think we're subversive. They allow us.

CONSPIRATOR B. They kill one of us, two more —

CONSPIRATOR A. Do you believe it?

CONSPIRATOR B. It's what you've always said.

CONSPIRATOR A. I don't know.

CONSPIRATOR B. You're overtired. Let's get some coffee.

CONSPIRATOR A. It's me.

CONSPIRATOR B. What is? What?

CONSPIRATOR A. I can't go on. I'm the spy.

CONSPIRATOR B. Not you.

CONSPIRATOR A. Everyone's under suspicion.

CONSPIRATOR B. But not you. Not really you.

CONSPIRATOR A. Yes.

CONSPIRATOR B. Always?

CONSPIRATOR A. Yes.

CONSPIRATOR B. When you recruited me?

CONSPIRATOR A. Yes.

CONSPIRATOR B. When you assassinated the duke?

CONSPIRATOR A. Yes.

CONSPIRATOR B. But you're the one we all depend on.

CONSPIRATOR A. Yes.

CONSPIRATOR B. I was just an ordinary villain. You explained. You said I could be a hero. And now what? What? All along? A spy all along? Michel's death? And Marc, not Marc? And Louis arrested last week, all you? But I'll tell the others. We'll kill you. Why did you tell me?

CONSPIRATOR A. I was tired.

CONSPIRATOR B. We'll kill you.

CONSPIRATOR A. You won't tell the others. I feel better now. Everyone has moments of weakness.

CONSPIRATOR B. Of course I'll tell. I can't protect you.

CONSPIRATOR A. I'm sorry I told you but it means I have to kill you. (*He has a gun.*)

CONSPIRATOR B. It doesn't.

CONSPIRATOR A. Yes.

CONSPIRATOR B. I won't tell.

CONSPIRATOR A. Sorry.

CONSPIRATOR B. Wait.

CONSPIRATOR A. Yes?

CONSPIRATOR B. Wait.

CONSPIRATOR A. Hurry.

CONSPIRATOR B. You'll laugh.

CONSPIRATOR A. What?

CONSPIRATOR B. You'll laugh. It's all right, old friend, it's all right. The police are as full of secrets as we are. To think I never knew. And you never knew.

CONSPIRATOR A. What?

CONSPIRATOR B. It's me too. I'm a police spy too. So you needn't kill me, all right? We just have to go on keeping each other's secret and doing our job. My dear old friend. I thought Michel and Marc and Louis were all my own work, and all the time it was you too. It is tiring, isn't it, the double life, twice as exhausting. What a relief to know. We'll never say another word about it, but we have each other now. We were always comrades, I always loved you, and how much more comrades now. How I love you now. Truth at last.

CONSPIRATOR A. But I was lying, you see.

CONSPIRATOR B. What?

CONSPIRATOR A. I'm not a spy.

CONSPIRATOR B. What?

CONSPIRATOR A. You are.

CONSPIRATOR B. What?

CONSPIRATOR A. Sorry. (*He raises the gun.*)

CONSPIRATOR B. What?

A beach. A group of MEN *are paddling in the sea, their trousers rolled up round their knees.* PIERRE *is sitting on the sand reading some files. He has a handkerchief on his head and is drinking a bottle of wine. The* MEN *in the sea chat and play.*

MEN. It's cold.
    No it's not cold.
    Mind the crab
    Ooh where?
    Don't splash
    Is that a jellyfish?

A HOLIDAYMAKER *approaches, carrying a book.*

HOLIDAYMAKER. Lovely day.

PIERRE. Lovely.

HOLIDAYMAKER. They're having fun.

PIERRE. Oh yes, they're good lads.

HOLIDAYMAKER. Nice picnic.

PIERRE. Care to join me?

HOLIDAYMAKER. Oh I didn't mean — well thank you very much.

He sits with PIERRE *and shares the wine.* PIERRE *is already slightly drunk and gets more so.*

Workers from the factory are they, having an outing?

PIERRE. I do bring workers to the seaside, yes. I also bring convicts.

HOLIDAYMAKER. Convicts are they? Now I come to look at them they have got sinister faces. You don't want to get convicts mixed up with ordinary people on a beach. I'm a respectable working man.

PIERRE. I do bring convicts, as part of their rehabilitation you see, and I also bring patients from the hospital.

HOLIDAYMAKER. Oh patients are they? Salt water do them good. Nothing contagious of course. More convalescent?

PIERRE. I do bring physically ill patients to the beach but I also bring mentally disturbed —

HOLIDAYMAKER. Oh, mental cases. That accounts for it. Very well behaved I must say for loonies.

PIERRE. I do bring —

HOLIDAYMAKER. Quite safe I suppose?

PIERRE. I know them all by name. I've turned a mob into individuals.

HOLIDAYMAKER. Come when they're called do they?

PIERRE. It's nice for them to have a day off out of the workshop. Don't worry, I keep an eye on them.

HOLIDAYMAKER. That's the thing. Keep an eye on them.

PIERRE. Very interesting cases some of them.

HOLIDAYMAKER. I like a good story.

PIERRE. That one over there with a long nose and close-set eyes.

HOLIDAYMAKER. Close-set eyes is a sure sign. And if your eyebrows meet.

PIERRE. He stirred up trouble at his place of work. Something about an association of workers. He resisted the police to such an extent the army had to be called in. Extremely violent criminal type, psychopath, paranoid fantasies, unhappy childhood, alcoholic father, inadequate mother —

HOLIDAYMAKER. Ah, that's often the way.

PIERRE. Extremely disorganised personality, with high blood pressure and low intelligence, a weak heart, anarchist literature, abnormal sexual proclivities, and cold feet due to inadequate circulation.

HOLIDAYMAKER. Responding to treatment is he?

PIERRE. Cries a good deal. Unemployable.

HOLIDAYMAKER. You must be a great comfort.

PIERRE. I do my best to understand him.

HOLIDAYMAKER (*shows his book*). I'm fascinated by criminal

literature. Ever read Arsène Lupin? High-class burglar in white gloves and a detective who's always after him. Takes your mind off things.

PIERRE. I used to want a garden you see.

HOLIDAYMAKER. I've got a small garden.

PIERRE. Flowering bushes. Where families would stroll on a Sunday. Iron cages high in the sky.

HOLIDAYMAKER. I like a garden.

PIERRE. Instead I've got a city. Whole city. All on the great panoptic principle.

One of the MEN *suddenly gives a cry and leaps to attack* PIERRE. *Before he reaches him there is a shot and the* MAN *falls.* PIERRE *jumps at the sound of the shot but is otherwise unperturbed. The other* MEN *stand frozen. Two* GUARDS *come and carry the dead* MAN *off.*

HOLIDAYMAKER. Good heavens!

PIERRE. Poor fellow. There's always a few. Fascinating case, I'm sorry to lose him. Never very happy.

HOLIDAYMAKER. Good heavens! Well. Was that a guard I suppose was it? Armed guard?

PIERRE. Very rarely necessary. I regard it as a failure.

HOLIDAYMAKER. Stands by does he, in case of trouble?

PIERRE *goes over to the* MEN, *who are still standing still.*

PIERRE. I'm sorry about that. Very inconsiderate of Legrand to spoil the afternoon for the rest of us. Did it startle you? It startled me. This is not what I — This is not what you — Isn't the sea pretty today? We've still another thirty-five minutes to enjoy ourselves.

The MEN *start to paddle and splash again.* PIERRE *slowly goes back and sits down with the* HOLIDAYMAKER.

HOLIDAYMAKER. Nasty shock for you.

PIERRE. I don't like loud noises.

HOLIDAYMAKER. Still it is a comfort to have that kind of protection.

PIERRE. I think so. Yes, I think so. Ultimately of course I hope — I'd like to see — well afternoons like this are so inspiring. Afternoons like this one was. The guard is inclined to over-react, he's only young. I must speak to the minister.

The HOLIDAYMAKER *takes a hipflask from his pocket.*

HOLIDAYMAKER. Here.

PIERRE *drinks. The* HOLIDAYMAKER *drinks. They sit in silence. The* HOLIDAYMAKER *passes the flask again.*

PIERRE. Mustn't have too much.

HOLIDAYMAKER. Bit of a shock.

PIERRE. Yes, but I —

PIERRE *takes the flask and drinks.*

The trouble is I have to make a speech. Later on. In front of the minister. He's going to lay the foundation stone. I'm always a little nervous at these official — I shall just explain quite simply how the criminals are punished, the sick are cured, the workers are supervised, the ignorant are educated, the unemployed are registered, the insane are normalised, the criminals — No, wait a minute. The criminals are supervised. The insane are cured. The sick are normalised. The workers are registered. The unemployed are educated. The ignorant are punished. No. I'll need to rehearse this a little. The ignorant are normalised. Right. The sick are punished. The insane are educated. The workers are cured. The criminals are cured. The unemployed are punished. The criminals are normalised. Something along those lines.

HOLIDAYMAKER. Lovely day out for them. Nice treat.

PIERRE *and the* HOLIDAYMAKER *drink. The* MEN *look at* PIERRE.

Fen

'It was work, work, work, it was all their lives.'
Retired School Teacher

'What's the point of working till you drop?'
Union Branch Secretary

'I'm the only Marxist in the Fens.'
Smallholder

'They must think I'm off the road.'
Smallholder

'If you don't believe, you don't see anything.'
Retired Landworker

Fen was first performed by the Joint Stock Theatre Group at the University of Essex Theatre on 20 January 1983 and opened at the Almeida Theatre, London on 16 February 1983, with the following cast:

SHIRLEY
SHONA
MISS CADE   } Linda Bassett
MARGARET

BOY
ANGELA
DEB   } Amelda Brown
MRS FINCH

JAPANESE BUSINESSMAN
NELL
MAY   } Cecily Hobbs
MAVIS

MRS HASSETT
BECKY
ALICE   } Tricia Kelly
IVY

VAL
GHOST   } Jennie Stoller

WILSON
FRANK
MR TEWSON   } Bernard Strother
GEOFFREY

Directed by Les Waters
Designed by Annie Smart
Lighting by Tom Donnellan
Original music by Ilona Sekacz

This play was written after a workshop in a village in the Fens.

Note on layout
A speech usually follows the one immediately before it BUT:
1. when one character starts speaking before the other has finished, the point of interruption is marked / .
eg. DEB: You shut up, / none of your business.
     MAY: Don't speak to your mum like that. etc

2   a character sometimes continues speaking right through
     another's speech.
eg. GEOFFREY: We had terrible times. If I had cracked tomatoes
     for my tea / I
     SHIRLEY: It's easy living here like I do now.
     GEOFFREY: thought I was lucky. etc

Production Note

From the workshop and from talking to Les Waters and Annie
Smart before I wrote the play, I had some idea of what the play
was like physically while I was writing it, and certain things are an
essential part of its structure: no interval, almost continuous
action (the scenes following with hardly a break), all furniture
and props on stage throughout and one set which doesn't change.
In the original production this was achieved by Annie Smart's
design of a field in a room, which was brilliant but which I can't
claim as part of the play as I wrote it.

   In the earlier edition there was a musical setting of lines from
Rilke's Duino Elegies, which was cut very early in the production.
Though I miss having two songs, the Girls' Song about particular
and limited wants and the Rilke about a vaster yearning, I do on
the whole prefer this version.

   I have kept the line near the end where the Boy from the
beginning of the play reappears and says 'Jarvis . . .' In practice
we cut it, as we wanted to keep Angela on stage and the parts
were doubled. But I like the idea that that boy was that old man,
so I've kept it, for reading anyway.

   May sings, ie she stands as if singing and we hear what she
would have liked to sing. So something amazing and beautiful —
she wouldn't sing unless she could sing like that. In the original
production it was a short piece of opera on tape.

As the audience comes in, a BOY from the last century, barefoot and in rags, is alone in a field, in a fog, scaring crows. He shouts and waves a rattle. As the day goes on his voice gets weaker till he is hoarse and shouting in a whisper. It gets dark.

Scene One

It gets lighter, but still some mist. It is the present. JAPANESE BUSINESSMAN, in suit, with camera.

JAPANESE BUSINESSMAN. Mr Takai, Tokyo Company, welcomes you to the fen. Most expensive earth in England. Two thousand pounds acre. Long time ago, under water. Fishes and eels swimming here. Not true people had webbed feet but did walk on stilts. Wild people, fen tigers. In 1630 rich lords planned to drain fen, change swamp into grazing land, far thinking men, brave investors. Fen people wanted to keep fishes and eels to live on, no vision. Refuse work on drainage, smash dykes, broke sluices. Many problems. But in the end we have this beautiful earth. Very efficient, flat land, plough right up to edge, no waste. This farm, one of our twenty-five farms, very good investment. Belongs to Baxter Nolesford Ltd, which belongs to Reindorp Smith Farm Land trust, which belongs 65% to our company. We now among many illustrious landowners, Esso, Gallagher, Imperial Tobacco, Equitable Life, all love this excellent earth. How beautiful English countryside. I think it is too foggy to take pictures. Now I find teashop, warm fire, old countryman to tell tales.

Scene Two

WOMEN *and a* BOY *working in a row, potato picking down a field. When their buckets are full they tip the potatoes into a potato grave at the top of the field.*

VAL *thirty,* ANGELA *twenty-eight,* SHIRLEY *fifty,* NELL *forty,* WILSON *sixteen.*

MRS HASSETT *forty-five, gangmaster, stands at the bottom of the field watching them. They pick down and back once, and start down again.*

SHIRLEY *sings the fireman's song from children's TV programme* Trumpton.

SHIRLEY (*sings*). Pugh, Pugh, Barney McGrew,
Cuthbert, Dibble, Grub.
Da da diddidi da
Diddidi diddidi diddidi da
Da da diddidi da
Diddidi diddidi da, pom.

ANGELA *joins in and sings with her.*

NELL *joins in.*

VAL *stops and stands staring.*

NELL. You all right, girl?

NELL *doesn't stop working.*

VAL *goes down the field to the end where* MRS HASSETT *is.*

MRS HASSETT. What's the matter, Val? Took short?

VAL. I've got to leave now.

MRS HASSETT. What do you mean, got to leave? It ent three o'clock.

VAL. I know, but I'm going.

MRS HASSETT. Who's going to do your work then? Mr Coleman wants this done today. How does it make me look?

VAL. Sorry, I can't help it.

MRS HASSETT. You think twice before you ask me for work again because I'll think twice an' all. So where you off to so fast?

VAL. Just back home.

MRS HASSETT. What's waiting there then?

VAL. I've got to. I've gone. Never mind.

MRS HASSETT. Wait then, I'll give you a lift halfway. I've another lot at Mason's I've got to look in on.

VAL. I've got to go now.

MRS. HASSETT. You'll be quicker waiting. I don't owe you nothing for today.

VAL. You do.

MRS HASSETT. Not with you messing me about like this, not if you want another chance.

VAL. I'll start walking and you pick me up.

VAL goes.

The others arrive at the end of the field. WILSON *is first.*

MRS HASSETT. What's your name? Wilson? The idea's to get the work done properly not win the Derby. Want to come again?

WILSON. Yes, Mrs Hassett.

MRS HASSETT. Because if you work regular with me it's done proper with stamps. I don't want you signing on at the same time because that makes trouble for me, never mind you. And if I catch you with them moonlighting gangs out of town you don't work for me again. Work for peanuts them buggers, spoil it for the rest of you, so keep well clear.

NELL. Spoil it for you, Mrs Hassett.

MRS HASSETT. Spoil it for all of us, Nell.

ANGELA. What's up with Val?

NELL. You've got two colour tellies to spoil.

MRS HASSETT. Think you'd get a better deal by yourself? Think you'd get a job at all?

ANGELA. Where's she gone? Ent she well?

MRS HASSETT. She don't say she's ill. She don't say what.

NELL. You paying her what she's done?

MRS HASSETT. Will you mind your own business or she won't be the only one don't get picked up tomorrow morning.

NELL. It is my business. You'd treat me the same.

ANGELA. Nell, do give over.

SHIRLEY. Come on, Nell, let's get on with it.

NELL. She treat you the same.

WILSON. If I do hers, do I get her money?

MRS HASSETT. You'll have enough to do to finish your own.

WILSON. Can I try?

MRS HASSETT. If you do it careful.

NELL. Am I crazy? Am I crazy? Am I crazy?

MRS HASSETT. I'm off now, ladies and gent. Can't stand about in this wind. I should get a move on, you've plenty to do.

ANGELA. Nell, you're just embarrassing.

MRS HASSETT *goes.* SHIRLEY *and* WILSON *have already started work.*

ANGELA *starts.*

NELL *starts.*

Scene Three

FRANK *thirty driving a tractor.*
Earphones. We can hear the music he's listening to.
The music fades down, we hear him talking to himself.

FRANK. Mr Tewson, Can I have a word with you?
Yes, Frank, what can I do for you lad?
I'm finding things a bit difficult.
So am I, Frank. Hard times.
Fellow come round from the union last week.
Little fellow with a squint?
I don't hold with strikes myself.

I'm not against the union, Frank. I can see the sense of it for
your big newfangle farms. Not when people are friends.
Fact is, Mr Tewson, living separate from the wife and kids I
can't seem to manage.
It's lucky I'm able to let them stay on in the cottage. The
council housing's not up to much eh?
I'm very grateful. But Mr Tewson I can't live on the money.
You'd get half as much again in a factory, Frank. I wouldn't
blame you. But I remember when your dad worked for my
dad and you and your brother played about the yard. Your
poor old brother, eh Frank? It was great we got him into that
home when your mum died. We're like family. We'd both put
up with a lot to go on living this good old life here.
I hate you, you old bugger.

FRANK *hits* MR TEWSON, *that is he hits himself across the
face.*

VAL *arrives with* DEB *nine and* SHONA *six. They have a
suitcase. She leaves them at the side of the field with the
suitcase and goes to speak to* FRANK. *She has to attract his
attention, shouting 'Frank! Frank!' He stops the tractor, takes
off the earphones.*

FRANK. What happened?

VAL. Suddenly came to me.

FRANK. What's wrong?

VAL. I'm leaving him. I'm going to London on the train, I'm
taking the girls, I've left him a note and that's it. You follow
us soon as you can. It's the only thing. New life.

FRANK. Where are you going to live?

VAL. We'll find somewhere together.

FRANK. How much money you got?

VAL. Fifty-six pounds. I'll get a job. I just want to be with you.

FRANK. I want to be with you, Val.

VAL. All right then.

FRANK. What am I supposed to do in London?

VAL. Where do you want to go? You say. I don't mind. You don't like it here. You're always grumbling about Mr Tewson.

FRANK. He's not a bad old boy.

VAL. He don't pay what he should.

FRANK. He was good to my brother.

VAL. I'm in a panic.

FRANK. Shall I see you tonight?

VAL. In London?

FRANK. Here.

VAL. How can I get out? I'm going crazy all this dodging about.

FRANK. Come and live with me. If you're ready to leave.

VAL. With the girls?

FRANK. With or without.

VAL. He'll never let me. He'll have them off me.

FRANK. Please do.

They kiss.

VAL. I suppose I go home now. Unpack.

She gets the CHILDREN *and they go.*

Scene Four

VAL *and* DEB.

VAL. You're to be a good girl Deb, and look after Shona. Mummy will come and see you all the time. You can come and see Mummy and Frank. Mummy loves you very much. Daddy loves you very much. I'll only be down the road.

DEB. I want to go on the train.

VAL. We will go on the train sometime. We can't go now. Mummy's got to go and live with Frank because I love him. You be a good girl and look after Shona. Daddy's going to look after you. And Nan's going to look after you. Daddy loves you very much. I'll come and see you all the time.

DEB. I want new colours.

VAL. You've still got your old ones, haven't you. Lucky we didn't go away, you've still got all your things.

DEB. I want new colours.

VAL. I'll get you some new colours. Mummy's sorry. Love you very much. Look after Shona.

Scene Five

VAL *and* FRANK *dance together. Old-fashioned, formal, romantic, happy.*

Scene Six

ANGELA *and* BECKY, *her stepdaughter, fifteen.*
    BECKY *is standing still.* ANGELA *has a cup of very hot water.*

ANGELA. You shouldn't let me treat you like this.

BECKY. Can I sit down now, Angela?

ANGELA. No, because you asked. Drink it standing up. And you didn't call me mum.

BECKY. You're not, that's why.

ANGELA. Wouldn't want to be the mother of a filthy little cow like you. Pity you didn't die with her. Your dad wishes you'd died with her. Now drink it quick.

   BECKY *takes the cup and drops it. She goes to pick it up.*

   Now look. Don't you dare pick it up. That's your trick is it, so I'll let you move? I'll have to punish you for breaking a cup. Why do you push me?

BECKY. Too hot.

   ANGELA *fills another cup from a kettle.*

ANGELA. It's meant to be hot. What you made of, girl? Ice cream? Going to melt in a bit of hot? I'll tell your dad what a bad girl you are if he phones up tonight and then he won't love you. He'll go off in his lorry one day and not come back and he'll send for me and he won't send for you. Say sorry and you needn't drink it.

BECKY *starts to drink it*.

Faster than that. Crybaby. Hurts, does it? Say sorry now. Sorry mummy.

BECKY *stands in silence*.

I'm not bothered. No one's going to come you know. No chance of anyone dropping in. We've got all afternoon and all evening and all night. We can do what we like so long as we get your dad's tea tomorrow.

BECKY. I'm going to tell him.

ANGELA. You tell him what you like and what won't I tell him about you.

BECKY. I'll tell someone. You'll be put in prison, you'll be burnt.

ANGELA. You can't tell because I'd kill you. You know that. Do you know that?

BECKY. Yes.

ANGELA. Do you?

BECKY. Yes.

ANGELA. Now why not say sorry and we'll have a biscuit and see what's on telly. You needn't say mummy, you can say, 'Sorry, Angela, I'm bad all through.' I don't want you driving me into a mood.

BECKY. Sorry, Angela, bad all through.

ANGELA *strokes* BECKY's *hair then yanks it*.

ANGELA. No stamina, have you? 'Sorry Angela.' What you made of, girl?

Scene Seven

NELL *is hoeing her garden.*
 BECKY, DEB, SHONA *spying on her.*

DEB. Is she a man?

BECKY. No, she's a morphrodite.

DEB. What's that?

BECKY. A man and a woman both at once.

DEB. Can it have babies by itself?

BECKY. It has them with another morphrodite. Like snails. But
 she's never met one yet.

SHONA. Is she a witch?

BECKY. She eats little children, so watch out.

DEB. She talks to herself. That's spells.

BECKY. Angela says she makes trouble.

DEB. She goes in the gang with my mum.

BECKY. She makes trouble.

DEB. Let's get her wild.

BECKY. I hate her, don't you?

DEB. She makes me feel sick.

BECKY. Let's make her shout.

SHONA. Poo bum! Poo bum!

DEB. Shut up, Shona.

NELL. What you doing there?

BECKY. Watching you, so what?

NELL. Come out and watch me close up then.

DEB. Can I ask you something?

NELL. What?

DEB. Have you got — have you got — ?

NELL. What?

They giggle.

NELL. Well I don't know what you want. Want to help me with my garden? You can do some weeding.

BECKY. That's a funny hat.

NELL. That's a good old hat. It's a funny old hat.

SHONA. Poo bum.

NELL. You watch out, Shona, or you'll have a smack.

DEB. You hit my sister and I'll kill you.

BECKY. I'll kill you. Kill you with the hoe. You're horrible.

BECKY *takes the garden hoe and pokes it at* NELL.

NELL. Watch what you're doing. Put it down.

DEB. Make her run. Give her a poke.

BECKY. Jump. Jump.

SHONA. Poo poo poo poo.

NELL. You stop that.

NELL *grabs* SHONA, *holds her in front of her, between herself and the hoe.*

Now you mind who you poke.

SHONA *screams and struggles.*

Give me my hoe and get on home.

DEB. You let her go.

BECKY. I'll have your foot. I'll have your eyes.

NELL. Right then, you stop in there like a little rabbit.

NELL *pushes* SHONA *into a rabbit hutch.*

SHONA. Let me out.

DEB. Kill her.

BECKY. Let her out.

NELL. Give me that hoe first. Now shut up, Shona, or I'll have you for tea.

DEB. Kill her.

BECKY *screams and stabs at* NELL, *who ducks and gets her hat knocked off.*

NELL. Now give me my hoe.

BECKY *gives her the hoe.*

Give me my hat.

BECKY *gives her the hat.*

And get out of my garden.

DEB. Shona.

NELL. What if I keep Shona an hour or two? Teach you a lesson.

DEB. Please let her go.

SHONA. Deb, get me out, I can't move, get me out.

NELL. Nasty, nasty children. What will you grow up like? Nasty. You should be entirely different. Everything. Everything.

NELL *lets* SHONA *out.*

You're the poo bum now, all rabbit business.

SHONA. Are you a witch?

NELL. No, I'm a princess. Now get out.

Girl's Song (BECKY, DEB, SHONA)
I want to be a nurse when I grow up
And I want to have children and get married.
But I don't think I'll leave the village when I grow up.

I'm never going to leave the village when I grow up even when I get married.
I think I'll stay in the village and be a nurse.

I want to be a hairdresser when I grow up or perhaps a teacher.
I don't really care if I get married or be a hairdresser.

I want to be a cook when I grow up.
If I couldn't be a cook I'd be a hairdresser.
But I don't really want to leave the village when I grow up.

I don't think much about what I want to be.
I don't mind housework.

I think I want to be a housewife until I think of another job.

When I grow up I'm going to be a nurse and if not a hairdresser.

I'm going to be a hairdresser when I grow up and if not a nurse.

Scene Eight

MAY, VAL's *mother, sixty, filling in a pools coupon.* DEB *and* SHONA *colouring.*

MAY. When the light comes down from behind the clouds it comes down like a ladder into the graveyards. And the dead people go up the light into heaven.

SHONA. Can you see them going up?

MAY. I never have. You look for them, my sugar.

A long silence.

DEB. Sing something, nan.

MAY. I can't sing, my sugar.

Silence.

SHONA. Go on, sing something.

MAY. I can't, I can't sing.

Silence.

SHONA. Mum can sing.

MAY. Yes, she's got a nice voice, Val.

DEB. Sing something.

Pause. MAY *seems about to sing.*

MAY. I can't sing, my sugar.

DEB. You're no good then, are you.

MAY. There's other things besides singing.

DEB. Like what?

Silence.

VAL *comes. They all go on with what they're doing.*

VAL. Hello, mum. Hello, Deb. Oh Deb, hello. Shona, Shona. What are you drawing? Can't I look?

MAY. They're telling me off because I can't sing. You can sing them something since you're here.

VAL. You want me to sing you something, Deb?

DEB. No.

VAL. Shona?

Pause.

VAL *starts to sing. She stops.*

MAY. How long is this nonsense going to last?

VAL. Don't.

MAY. I'm ashamed of you.

VAL. Not in front.

MAY. What you after? Happiness? Got it have you? Bluebird of happiness? Got it have you? Bluebird?

Silence.

What you after?

DEB. Shut up.

VAL. Don't speak to your nan like that.

DEB. You shut up, / none of your business.

MAY. Don't speak to your mum like that. She's getting dreadful, Val. / You've only yourself to blame.

DEB. I'm not. You are. You're getting dreadful.

MAY. You see what I mean.

VAL. You're winding her up.

MAY. I'm winding her up? She was good as gold till you come in. / You better think what you're doing.

VAL. Don't start on me. Just because you had nothing.

MAY. Don't speak to me like that, / my girl, or it's out you go.

DEB. Don't speak to my mum.

VAL. I've not been here / five minutes.

DEB. Don't speak to my nan.

VAL. Shut up, Deb.

MAY. Don't speak to the child like that.

SHONA *screams and runs off. Silence.*

Don't go after her.

VAL. Don't you go after her.

MAY. Deb, you go and look after your sister.

DEB. No.

Pause.

VAL. I'd better go after her.

DEB. Leave her alone.

MAY. Leave her alone a bit, best thing.

Silence.

VAL. Never mind, Deb.

MAY. Get one thing straight. It's no trouble having them. They've always a place here.

VAL. I know that.

MAY. I'll stand by you. I stand by my children.

Silence.

I'd never have left you, Val.

VAL. Just don't.

MAY. I'd go through fire. What's stronger than that?

VAL. Just don't.

MAY. What's stronger?

Silence.

DEB. I'll get Shona.

Scene Nine

MR TEWSON *fifty-five farmer, and* MISS CADE, *thirty-five, from the City.*

TEWSON. Suppose I was to die. I can claim fifty percent working farmer relief on my land value.

CADE. And thirty percent on the value of your working capital.

TEWSON. My son would still have a bill of —

CADE. Three hundred thousand pounds.

TEWSON. Which I don't have.

CADE. That's the position exactly.

TEWSON. It would mean selling a hundred and fifty acres.

CADE. That's what it would mean.

TEWSON. He could do that.

CADE. It's certainly an option.

TEWSON. Take a good few generations before the whole farm disappears. Eh?

CADE. Alternatively you can give land direct to the Inland Revenue.

Pause.

Alternatively.

TEWSON. I need to be bloody immortal. Then I'd never pay tax. You're bloody immortal, eh? City institutions are immortal.

CADE. The farmers who have sold to us are happy, Mr Tewson.

TEWSON. Bloody driven to it. Don't have to like you as well. I've read about you, Miss Cade. Moguls.

CADE. The popular farming press unfortunately —

TEWSON. And tycoons. And barons.

CADE. The specialist journals take a longer view.

TEWSON. Who pushed the price of land up?

CADE. Not in fact the City.

TEWSON. I don't want these fields to be worth hundreds of thousands. More tax I have to pay.

CADE. We follow the market. The rise in prices is caused by government policies. Ever since the Heath administration introduced rollover relief —

TEWSON. Same old fields. My great great grandfather, Miss Cade.

Pause.

I am a member of the Country Landowners Association. We have ears in the corridors of power. My family are landowners. If I sell to you I become a tenant on my grandfather's land. Our president appealed to us to keep our nerve.

CADE. With us, your grandson will farm his grandfather's acres. The same number of acres. More. You'll have the capital to reinvest. Land and machinery.

Pause.

TEWSON. My family hold this land in trust for the nation.

CADE. We too have a sense of heritage.

Pause.

TEWSON. Grandson, eh?

CADE. No reason why not.

TEWSON. When I say nation. You don't want to go too far in the public responsibility direction. You raise the spectre of nationalisation.

CADE. No danger of that. Think of us as yourself.

TEWSON. No problem getting a new tractor then.

CADE. I can leave the papers with you.

TEWSON. Cup of tea? Daresay Mrs Tewson's made a cake. You want to watch the Transport and General Workers. The old agricultural union was no trouble. We'll have these buggers stopping the trains.

MISS CADE *goes.* TEWSON *is following her. He is stopped by the sight of a* WOMAN *working in the fields. She is as real as the other women workers but barefoot and wearing nineteenth century rags. She is a* GHOST.

TEWSON. Good afternoon. Who's that? You're not one of Mrs Hassett's girls.

GHOST. We are starving, we will not stand this no longer. Rather than starve we are torment to set you on fire. You bloody farmers could not live if it was not for the poor, tis them that keep you bloody rascals alive, but there will be a slaughter made amongst you very soon. I should very well like to hang you the same as I hanged your beasts. You bloody rogue, I will light up a little fire for you the first opportunity I can make.

TEWSON. My father saw you. I didn't believe him.

GHOST. I been working in this field a hundred and fifty years. There ain't twenty in this parish but what hates you, bullhead.

TEWSON. Are you angry because I'm selling the farm?

GHOST. What difference will it make?

TEWSON. None, none, everything will go on the same.

GHOST. That's why I'm angry.

TEWSON. I'm going.

GHOST. Get home then. I live in your house. I watch television with you. I stand beside your chair and watch the killings. I watch the food and I watch what makes people laugh. My baby died starving.

Scene Ten

WOMEN *onion packing*. SHIRLEY, NELL, ANGELA, ALICE, *a Baptist, 35. They have a large box of onions which they pack a few at a time in small bags for the supermarket, discarding those that don't make the grade. They keep working hard throughout the scene, including* NELL.

SHIRLEY. No Val today?

ANGELA. No time for onions.

NELL. Need the money though, won't she?

ALICE. Not surprised she don't come. You shouldn't be surprised.

SHIRLEY. What's that mean?

ALICE. Way you treat her.

SHIRLEY. What's that mean?

ALICE. Everyone's acting funny with her.

ANGELA. She's the one acting funny. Leave her own kiddies. If I had my own kiddies I wouldn't leave them.

ALICE. I know she's wicked but she's still my friend.

SHIRLEY. What you talking about wicked?

ALICE. It was sinners Jesus Christ come for so don't you judge.

SHIRLEY. Who said anything?

ALICE. Outside school yesterday, collecting time, no one said hello except me.

SHIRLEY. I wasn't there, was I. Expect me to shout from the other end of the street. Hello Val! Say hello now, shall I? Hello, Val! That'll cheer her up wherever she is. Altogether now, Hello —

ALICE. Never mind. You're all so — never mind.

NELL. Did I ever tell you about my grandfather?

SHIRLEY. When he was a boy and run away, that one?

NELL. I know you know, you'll have to hear it again.

ALICE. People are all miserable sinners. Miserable.

SHIRLEY. You want to tell Val not us. Give her a fright.

ANGELA. This one of your dirty stories, Nell? Or one of your frightening ones?

SHIRLEY. It's funny.

NELL. He used to swear this really happened. When he was ten his mother died in childbirth, and his father soon got a woman in he said was a housekeeper, but she slept with him from the first night. My grandfather hated her and she hated him, and she'd send him to bed without any tea, and his father always

took her side. So after a few months of this, early one morning
when his father had gone to work but she wasn't up yet, he
took some bread and some cold tea and he run off. He walked
all day and it got real dark and he was frit as hell. There was
no houses on the road, just an old green drove sometimes
going off towards the coast, so he thought he'd have to sleep
by the road. Then he sees a little light shining so he set off
down the drove that led to it and he comes to an old stone
house. So he knocks on the door and the woman comes, and
she'd a candlestick in one hand and a big old copper stick in the
other. But when she sees it's only a boy she says come in and
she makes him sit by the fire and gives him a bowl of hot milk
with some fat bacon in it and a hunk of brown bread. Then
she says, 'Me and my husband are going out but you can sleep
by the fire. But you must stay here in the kitchen,' she says,
'whatever you do, you mustn't go through that door,' and she
points to the door at the back of the kitchen. Then her
husband came and said the pony trap was ready and he didn't
look too pleased to see the boy but he didn't say nothing and
off they went for their night out. So he sat by the fire and sat
by the fire, and he thought I'll just take a look through that
door. So he turned the handle but it was locked. And he saw a
key lay on the dresser and he tried it and slowly opened the
door, and then he wished he hadn't. There was a candle in the
window which was the light he'd seen, and a long table, and on
the table was a coffin with the lid off, and inside the coffin
there was a body. And he was just going to shut the door and
hurry back by the fire when the body in the coffin sat up and
opened its eyes, and said, 'Who are you boy?' Oh he were
petrified. But the body said, 'Don't be afraid, I'm not dead,'
he said, 'Where have they gone?' meaning the woman and the
husband. When he heard they were out he got out of the
coffin and come in the kitchen and made some cocoa. Then he
told my grandfather his missus had been having an affair with
the chap from the next smallholding, and she was trying to get
rid of him by putting rat poison in his food, and he'd fed it to
some pigeons and they'd died. So what he'd done, he'd
pretended to die, and she'd told the doctor he'd had a heart
attack, and he'd been put in the coffin. And before that he'd

sold the farm without telling the wife and had the money safe in the bank under another name. So he give my grandfather a screwdriver and said when the couple came home and screwed down the coffin, after they was in bed he was to unscrew it again. So he went back by the fire and pretended to be asleep, and he heard them screw up the coffin and laughing about how they'd got the old man's farm and kissing, and later he got the old fellow out and he were real glad because he said he wanted a pee so bad he could almost taste it. Then he got a large two tined pitchfork and a pickaxe handle and he said 'Come on it's time to go.' My grandfather thought they were going to leave, but the old fellow crept upstairs, and gave the boy the candle and the pickaxe handle to carry, and he crept up and opened the door of the bedroom. There was the couple lying close together, completely naked and fast asleep. Then suddenly he raised the pitchfork and brung it down as hard as he could directly over their bare stomachs, so they were sort of stitched together. They screamed and screamed and he grabbed the pickaxe handle off of my grandfather and clubbed them on their heads till they lay still. Then he gets the man and takes him downstairs and puts him in the coffin and screws it up. He says, 'They'll bury him tomorrow and think it's me, and when they find her dead they'll know she was out drinking with her fellow and they'll think he killed her and done a bunk, so the police won't be looking for me,' he said, 'they'll be looking for him. And I'm going to start a new life in London or Australia, and if you talk about it I'll find you and slit your throat from ear to ear.' And he never did till he was so old he knew the old man must be dead, and even then he waited a good few years more, and I was the first person he ever told. The old fellow gave my grandfather a gold sovereign and told him to walk west and look for a job on a farm over that way, so he walked five days and slept five nights in barns, and got a job on a farm near Doncaster.

ANGELA. He never heard no more about it?

NELL. If it was in the paper he wouldn't know because he couldn't read. He never heard nothing about it, and his father never found him neither.

ALICE. You said it was funny, Shirley.

ANGELA. I don't reckon it's true.

SHIRLEY. Funny if it is true, eh Nell?

NELL. I believe it all right. Why not? There's harder things to believe than that. Makes me laugh.

Scene Eleven

SHIRLEY *working in the house. She goes from one job to another, ironing, mending, preparing dinner, minding a baby.* VAL *is there, not doing anything.* SHIRLEY *never stops throughout the scene.*

VAL. I made a cake Deb always likes and I had to throw half of it away. Frank and I don't like cake.

SHIRLEY. You're bound to miss them.

VAL. I do see them.

Silence.

It's right he should keep them. I see that. It's not his fault. He's a good father. It's better for them to stay in their own home. Frank's only got the one room. It makes sense. It's all for the best.

SHIRLEY. At harvest dad'd say, 'Come on, Shirley, you're marker.' Then if the shock fell over, 'Who's the marker?' I'd say, 'I'll go outside, let someone else be marker,' but he wouldn't let me. And leading the horse. 'What if he treads on my feet?' I never could work in front of a horse. Many's the time they'd bolt up the field. My mother wouldn't let me off. 'Just get on with it, Shirley.'

VAL. Can I help with something?

SHIRLEY. Thank you but I know how I like it.

Silence.

VAL. Is that Mary's baby?

SHIRLEY. No, it's Susan's.

VAL. You've so many grandchildren I lose track.

SHIRLEY. I'll be a great-grandmother next.

VAL. What, Sukey's never?

SHIRLEY. No, but she's sixteen now and I was a grandmother at thirty-two.

Silence.

Same thing when I went into service. I was fifteen and I hated it. They had me for a week's trial and I could have gone home at the end of it but I didn't want my mother to think she'd bred a gibber. Stayed my full year.

Silence.

I don't think she will somehow, Sukey. She's got green hair. Shocks her mother.

Silence.

Woken up, have we?

SHIRLEY *picks up the baby.*

VAL. I can't remember what they look like.

SHIRLEY. You see them every other day.

VAL. I don't think I can have looked at them when I had them. I was busy with them all the time so I didn't look. Now when I meet them I really stare. But they're not the same.

SHIRLEY. You've too much time on your hands. You start thinking. Can't think when you're working in the field can you? It's work work work, then you think, 'I wonder what the time is,' and it's dinnertime. Then you work again and you think, 'I wonder if it's time to go home,' and it is. Mind you, if I didn't need the money I wouldn't do any bugger out of a job.

VAL. Sukey's a freak round here but if she went to a city she wouldn't be, not so much. And I wouldn't.

SHIRLEY. You can take the baby off me if you want to do something.

VAL *takes the baby.*

SHIRLEY. We have to have something to talk about, Val, you
    mustn't mind if it's you. We'll soon stop. Same things people
    do in cities get done here, we're terrible here, you're the latest
    that's all. If it's what you want, get on with it. Frank left his
    wife two years ago and everyone's got used to that. What I
    can't be doing with is all this fuss you're making.

VAL. I can't hold the baby, it makes me cry. I'll do the ironing.

SHIRLEY. Give her here then. You don't want to be so soft. If
    you can't stop away from them, go back to them.

VAL. I can't leave Frank.

SHIRLEY (*to the baby*). Nothing's perfect is it, my poppet?
    There's a good girl.

   SHIRLEY's *husband* GEOFFREY, *sixty, comes in. By the end
   of the scene he has had the soup she prepared.*

GEOFFREY. Dinner ready?

SHIRLEY. Just about.

VAL. Hello, Geoffrey.

GEOFFREY. Could do with some dinner.

SHIRLEY. Ent you got a civil tongue?

GEOFFREY. I don't hold you personally responsible, Val.
    You're a symptom of the times. Everything's changing,
    everything's going down. Strikes, militants, I see the Russians
    behind it. / All the boys want to do today

SHIRLEY. You expect too much Val. Till Susan was fifteen I
    never went out. Geoffrey wouldn't either, he wouldn't go to
    the pub without me. 'She's mine as much as yours', he says,

GEOFFREY. is drive their bikes and waste petrol. When we went
    to school we got beaten and when we got home we got beaten
    again. They don't want to work today.

SHIRLEY. 'I've as much right to stop in as what you have.'
    Pause.
    Lived right out on the fen till ten years ago. You could stand

at the door with your baby in your arms and not see a soul
from one week's end to the next. / Delivery van come once a
week. My sister come at Christmas.

GEOFFREY. Don't talk to me about unemployment. They've
got four jobs. Doing other people out of jobs. Being a
horseman was proper work, but all your Frank does is sit on a
tractor. Sitting down's not work. Common market takes all
the work.

Pause.

Only twenty in church on Sunday. Declining morals all round.
Not like in the war. Those French sending rockets to the
Argies, forgotten what we did for them I should think. /
Common market's a good thing for stopping wars.

SHIRLEY. I remember dad said to mum one Bank Holiday, 'Do
you want to go out?' 'Yes please,' she said. 'Right,' he said,
'We'll go and pick groundsel.'

GEOFFREY. We had terrible times. If I had cracked tomatoes for
my tea / I thought I was lucky. So why shouldn't you have

SHIRLEY. It's easy living here like I do now.

GEOFFREY. terrible times? Who are all these people / who come
and live

SHIRLEY. Your bike'd be mud right up to the middle of the
wheel.

GEOFFREY. here to have fun? I don't know anybody. Nobody
does. Makes me wild. / My mother was glad she could

SHIRLEY. I'd think, 'If anything's after me it'll have to pedal.'

GEOFFREY. keep us alive, that's all. I'm growing Chinese
radishes. I've never eaten Chinese food and I never will. Friend
of mine grows Japanese radishes and takes them to Bradford,
tries to sell them to the Pakis. Pakis don't want them. You
want to pull yourself together, girl, that's what you want to do.

Scene Twelve

WOMEN *working down the field, stone picking. Bad weather.*
SHIRLEY, VAL, ANGELA, BECKY, NELL.

SHIRLEY (*sings*). Who would true valour see
Let him come hither.
One here will constant be
Come wind come weather.
There's no discouragement
Shall make him once relent
His first avowed intent
To be a pilgrim.

*It's hard singing in the wind. She's out of breath. No one joins
in. They go on working silently. A military jet flies over, very
loud. Only NELL looks up, angry.*

They go on working.

MR TEWSON *comes out to watch.*

NELL. Sod this.

ANGELA. Keep up, Beck.

They reach the end of the field one by one and stop.

TEWSON. You're good workers, I'll say that for you.

NELL. Thank you very much.

TEWSON. Better workers than men. I've seen women working in
my fields with icicles on their faces. I admire that.

SHIRLEY. Better than men all right.

NELL. Bloody fools, that's all.

ANGELA. What you crying for, Beck?

BECKY. I'm not.

SHIRLEY. Cold are you?

BECKY. No.

NELL. I am and so are you. What's going to make us feel better?
Sun going to come out? You going to top yourself, Tewson,
like that farmer over Chatteris?

TEWSON. She's funny in the head, isn't she.

ANGELA. She likes a joke.

TEWSON. Better watch her tongue.

SHIRLEY. She's a good worker, Mr Tewson, she don't do no harm.

NELL. Don't I though. Don't I do harm. I'll do you some harm one of these days, you old bugger.

ANGELA. What you made of, Becky?

SHIRLEY. You'll get used to it.

BECKY. I want to be a hairdresser.

TEWSON. That was a friend of mine you were speaking of. He found out he had six months to live. So he sold his orchards without telling anyone. Then before he started to suffer he took his life. Never said a word to his family. Carried it out alone, very bravely. I think that's a tragedy.

SHIRLEY. Well it is, yes.

TEWSON. Might clear up tonight.

TEWSON *goes.*

NELL. Best hope if they all top themselves. Start with the queen and work down and I'll tell them when to stop.

VAL *has only now finished her piece and joins them.*

SHIRLEY. All right, Val?

NELL. What's wrong with you?

VAL. Nothing.

NELL. Slows you up a lot for nothing.

VAL. It's like thick nothing. I can't get on. Makes my arms and legs heavy.

SHIRLEY. Still you're back with the kids, best thing. Just get on with it.

VAL *starts working again.*

NELL. You think I'm the loony. Is she eating? Sleeping?

ANGELA. She wants to go to the doctor, get some valium. (*She calls after* VAL:) A man's not worth it, mate. Kids neither.

NELL. I'm not working in this.

SHIRLEY. Don't be soft.

NELL. It's more than rain, it's splinters. Come on, Becky, you've had enough.

BECKY. Can I stop, Angela? Please, mum, can I?

ANGELA. I've had enough myself. Can't work in this.

SHIRLEY. I can.

NELL, ALICE, BECKY *move off.* SHIRLEY *starts working again.* VAL *works too, slower.*

Scene Thirteen

FRANK *and* VAL.

FRANK. What?

VAL. I wanted to see you.

FRANK. Why?

Silence.

Coming back to me?

VAL. No.

FRANK. Then what? What?

Silence.

I don't want to see you, Val.

VAL. No.

FRANK. Stay with me tonight.

Silence.

VAL. No.

FRANK. Please go away.

Scene Fourteen

Baptist women's meeting. MRS FINCH, *40, the minister's wife, is taking the meeting.* MAVIS *and* MARGARET, *thirties, are two of the congregation. Happy, loving. They are singing when* VAL *and* ALICE *arrive. Song: 'He's Our Lord'.*

MRS FINCH. God is doing wonderful things among us.

MAVIS. I hope you'll stay with us because we all love each other.

ALICE. She's a friend of mine. I brought her.

MAVIS. Alice is a beautiful friend to have.

They sing: 'Thank you Jesus'.

ALICE *puts her arm round* VAL. MRS FINCH *comforts* VAL *too.* VAL *likes this.*

MRS FINCH. How lovely to be here again with all my sisters. And specially lovely to welcome new faces. We hope you will commit yourself to the Lord because with him you will have everything. And without him, nothing. This is not a perfect world and we can't be perfect in it. You know how we work cleaning our houses or weeding our gardens, but they're never perfect, there's always another job to start again. But our Lord Jesus is perfect, and in him we are made perfect. That doesn't mean I'm perfect. You know I'm not. I know you're not. But we've plunged ourselves body and soul in the water of God. Next Sunday Margaret will be baptised and she'll testify before the whole congregation. Tonight she's going to share with her loving sisters how she accepted the Lord into her life.

MARGARET. I thought I would be nervous but I'm not. Because Jesus is giving me strength to speak. I don't know where to begin because I've been unhappy as long as I can remember. My mother and father were unhappy too. I think my grandparents were unhappy. My father was a violent man. You'd hear my mother, you'd say, 'Are you all right, mum?' But that's a long time ago. I wasn't very lucky in my marriage. So after that I was on my own except I had my little girl. Some of you knew her. But for those of you who didn't, she couldn't see. I thought at first that was why she couldn't learn things but it turned out to be in her head as well. But I taught her to walk, they said she wouldn't but she did. She slept in my bed, she wouldn't let me turn away from her, she'd put her hand on my face. It was after she died I started drinking, which has been my great sin and brought misery to myself and those who love me. I betrayed them again and again by saying I would give it up, but the drink would have me hiding a little away. But my loving sisters in Christ stood by me. I thought if God wants me he'll give me a sign, because I couldn't believe he really would want someone as terrible as me. I thought if I hear two words today, one beginning with M for Margaret, my name, and one with J for Jesus, close together, then I'll know how close I am to him. And that very afternoon I was at Mavis's house and her little boy was having his tea, and he said, 'More jam, mum.' So that was how close Jesus was to me, right inside my heart. That was when I decided to be baptised. But I slid back and had a drink again and next day I was in despair. I thought God can't want me, nobody can want me. And a thrush got into my kitchen. I thought if that bird can fly out, I can fly out of my pain. I stood there and watched, I didn't open another window, there was just the one window open. The poor bird beat and beat round the room, the tears were running down my face. And at last as it found the window and went straight through into the air. I cried tears of joy because I knew Jesus would save me. / So I went to Malcolm and said 'Baptise me now because I'm ready'. I want to give myself over completely to God so there's nothing else of me left, and then the pain will be gone and I'll be saved. Without the love of my sisters I would never have got through.

VAL. I want to go.

ALICE. What? Val?

VAL. I'm going. You needn't.

ALICE. Aren't you well?

VAL. I feel sick.

ALICE. I'm coming, I'm coming.

VAL *and* ALICE *leave.*

They are outside alone. Night.

ALICE. It's a powerful effect.

VAL. Yes.

ALICE. I'm glad I brought you, Val.

VAL. I hated it.

ALICE. What do you mean?

VAL. That poor woman.

ALICE. She's all right now, thank the Lord.

VAL. She just liked a drink. No wonder. Can't you understand her wanting a drink?

ALICE. Of course I can. So can Jesus. That's why he forgives her.

VAL. She thinks she's rubbish.

ALICE. We're all rubbish but Jesus still loves us so it's all right.

VAL. It was kind of you to bring me. I loved the singing. And everyone was so loving.

ALICE. Well then? That's it, isn't it? Better than we get every day, isn't it? How cold everyone is to each other? All the women there look after each other. I was dreadful after the miscarriage and they saved my life. Let Jesus help you, Val, because I know you're desperate. You need to plunge in. What else are you going to do? Poor Val.

ALICE *hugs* VAL.

VAL. Can't you give me a hug without Jesus?

ALICE. Of course not, we love better in Jesus.

VAL. I'd rather take valium.

Scene Fifteen

VAL *and* FRANK.

VAL. I was frightened.

FRANK. When?

VAL. When I left you.

FRANK. I was frightened when you came back.

VAL. Are you now?

FRANK. Thought of killing myself after you'd gone. Lucky I
didn't.

VAL. What are you frightened of?

FRANK. Going mad. Heights. Beauty.

VAL. Lucky we live in a flat country.

Scene Sixteen

IVY's *birthday*. IVY, *ninety*, MAY's *mother*. MAY, DEB,
SHONA.
> *They sing 'Happy Birthday' — 'dear mum' 'dear greatnan.'*

IVY. Sometimes I think I was never there. You can remember a
thing because someone told you. When they were dredging the
mud out of the leat. I can picture the gantry clear as a bell.
But whether I was there or someone told me, I don't know.
Am I ninety? Ninety is it? 'Are you the bloody union man?'
he'd say to Jack. 'Are you the bloody union man?' And Jack'd
say, 'Are you going to pay him, because if not I'll splash it all
over.'

MAY. Kiss your greatnan, Shona.

IVY. Ever kill a mouse, Shona? Tuppence a score. How old are
you?

SHONA. Six.

IVY. I come home late from school on purpose so I wouldn't
have to help mum with the beet. So I had to go without my
tea and straight out to the field. 'You can have tea in the
dark,' mum said, 'but you can't pick beet in the dark.' I were
six then. Jack didn't wear shoes till he were fourteen. You
could stick a pin in. Walked through the night to the union
meeting. Fellow come round on his bike and made his speech
in the empty street and everybody'd be in the house listening
because they daren't go out because what old Tewson might

say. 'Vote for the blues, boys,' he'd say and he'd give them money to drink. They'd pull off the blue ribbons behind the hedge. Still have the drink though. You'd close your eyes at night, it was time to open them in the morning. Jack'd be out in the yard at midnight. 'It's my tilley lamp and my wick,' I said, 'you owe me for that, Mr Tewson.' Chased him with a besom. 'You join that union, Jack,' I said. Nothing I couldn't do then. Now my balance takes me and I go over backwards.

There was five of us if you count my brother John that had his face bit off by the horse. 'Are you the bloody union man?' That quack who said he could cure cancer. Took the insides of sheep and said it was the cancer he got out. I didn't believe it but most of them did. Stoned the doctor's house when he drove him out. Welcomed him back with a brass band. Laudanum pills were a great thing for pain. Walk from Littleport to Wisbech in no time.

Ninety is it? Old fellow lived next to us, he was a hundred. He'd come out on the bank and shout out to the undertaker lived on the other side, 'Jarvis, Jarvis, come and make my coffin.' 'Are you the bloody union man?' he'd say. 'Yes I am,' he'd say, 'and what about it?' They don't marry today with the same love. 'Jarvis, come and make my coffin.'

Scene Seventeen

VAL *and* FRANK. *Outdoors. Night.*

FRANK. What you doing?

VAL. Can't sleep.

FRANK. Come back to bed. I can't sleep with you up.

VAL. I'm not too bad in the day, am I?

FRANK. Go back to them then.

VAL. Tried that.

FRANK. He'd have you back still.

VAL. Tried it already.

FRANK. If I went away it might be easier. We'd know it was for
definite.

VAL. You could always come back. I'd come after you.

FRANK. I'd better kill myself hadn't I. Be out of your way then.

VAL. Don't be stupid.

FRANK. The girls are all right, you know.

VAL. I just want them. I can't help it. I just want them.

FRANK. I left my family.

VAL. Not for me.

FRANK. I didn't say it was for you. I said I manage.

VAL. I'm the one who should kill themself. I'm the one can't get
used to how things are. I can't bear it either way, without
them or without you.

FRANK. Try and get them off him again.

VAL. We've been over that. They're his just as much. Why should
he lose everything? He's got the place. We've been over that.

FRANK. Let's go to bed. I'm cold.

VAL. One of us better die I think.

Scene Eighteen

WOMEN *playing darts in the pub.* SHIRLEY, ALICE, ANGELA,
NELL.

    FRANK *alone. He is joined by* NELL.

NELL. How's Mr Tewson then?

    FRANK *doesn't answer.*

    You're his right-hand man.

FRANK. I do my job.

NELL. I'm nobody's right hand. And proud of it. I'm their left
foot more like. Two left feet.

FRANK. Bloody trouble-maker.

NELL. I just can't think like they do. I don't know why. I was brought up here like everyone else. My family thinks like everyone else. Why can't I? I've tried to. I've given up now. I see it all as rotten. What finished me off was my case. Acton's that closed down.

FRANK. Made trouble there.

NELL. I wanted what they owed me — ten years I'd topped their effing carrots. You all thought I was off the road. You'll never think I'm normal now. Thank God, eh?

NELL *goes to play darts.*

ANGELA *joins* FRANK.

ANGELA. All alone?

FRANK. Just having a pint.

ANGELA. How's Val?

FRANK. Fine.

ANGELA. Never thought you were the type.

FRANK. What type?

ANGELA. After the married women.

FRANK. I'm not.

ANGELA. I got married too soon you know. I think forty-five's a good age to get married. Before that you want a bit of fun. You having fun?

FRANK. No.

ANGELA. Maybe it's gone on too long.

FRANK. Should never have started.

ANGELA. You can always try again.

FRANK. Too late for that.

ANGELA. You've got no spirit, Frank. Nobody has round here. Flat and dull like the landscape. I am too. I want to live in the country.

FRANK. What's this then?

ANGELA. I like more scenery. The Lake District's got scenery. We went there on our honeymoon. He said we were going to live in the country. I wouldn't have come. Real country is romantic. Away from it all. Makes you feel better.

FRANK. This is real country. People work in it. You want a holiday.

ANGELA. I want more than two weeks. You wouldn't consider running away with me?

FRANK. I'm thinking of killing myself.

ANGELA. God, so am I, all the time. We'll never do it. We'll be two old dears of ninety in this pub and never even kissed each other.

ANGELA *goes back to the darts*.

NELL *talks to* FRANK *again*.

NELL. Tell you something about Tewson. He's got a sticker in the back of his car, Buy British Beef. And what sort of car is it?

FRANK. Opel.

NELL. There, see?

FRANK. He's sold the farm, hasn't he? He's just a tenant himself. He had to, to get money for new equipment.

NELL. So who's boss? Who do you have a go at? Acton's was Ross, Ross is Imperial Foods, Imperial Foods is Imperial Tobacco, so where does that stop? He's your friend, I know that. Good to your brother, all that. Nice old fellow.

FRANK. That's right.

NELL. You don't think I'm crackers, do you?

FRANK. No.

NELL. I don't think you are neither. You cheer up anyway. Don't give them the satisfaction.

FRANK. I'm fine, thank you.

NELL. You never see a farmer on a bike.

Scene Nineteen

ANGELA *and* BECKY. ANGELA *has an exercise book of* BECKY's.

BECKY. It's private.

ANGELA. Nothing's private from me.

BECKY. Give it back.

ANGELA. Ashamed of it? I should think so. It's rubbish. And it's dirty. And it doesn't rhyme properly. Listen to this.

BECKY. No.

ANGELA. You're going to listen to this, Becky. You wrote it, you hear it. (*She reads:*)

When I'm dead and buried in the earth
Everyone will cry and be sorry then.
Nightingales will sing and wolves will howl.
I'll come back and frighten you to death.

Who? Me, I suppose. Me?

BECKY. No.

ANGELA. Who?

BECKY. Anyone.

ANGELA. Me, but you won't. You've got a horrible mind. (*She reads:*)

The saint was burnt alive
The crackling fat ran down.
Everyone ran to hear her scream
They thought it was a bad dream.

Eugh.
Oh this is very touching. (*She reads:*)

Mother where are you sweet and dear?
Your lonely child is waiting here.

BECKY. No, no, shut up.

ANGELA. If you could see what's done to me
You'd come and get me out of here. /

My love for you is always true —

BECKY. Mother where are you sweet and dear?
Your lonely child is waiting here.
If you could see what's done to me /
You'd come and get me out of here.
My love for you is always true
Mother mother sweet and dear.

ANGELA. You shut up, Becky. I never said you could. Becky I'm
warning you. Just for that you've got to hear another one. Not
a word. Now this is dirty. Wrote this in bed I expect. (*She
reads*:)

He pressed her with a passionate embrace
Tears ran down all over her face.
He put his hand upon her breast
Which gave her a sweet rest.
He put his hand upon her cunt
And put his cock up her.

That doesn't even rhyme, you filthy child.

He made love to her all night long.
They listened to the birdsong.

What puts filth like that into your head? What if I showed
your dad?

BECKY. No.

ANGELA. Lucky I'm your friend.

BECKY. I'll never do another one.

ANGELA. I don't care. Hope you don't. You should do one for
Frank.

BECKY. I don't love Frank.

ANGELA. You love Frank, do you? I hadn't guessed that.

BECKY. I don't. I said I don't. You do.

ANGELA. What? Watch out, Becky, don't get me started. Make a
poem about him dying.

BECKY. He's not dead?

ANGELA. He tried to. He took some pills, but Val got the ambulance.

BECKY. When? When?

ANGELA. I'll make one.

> Frank was miserable and wished he was dead.
> He had horrible thoughts in his head.
> He took some pills to end his life.
> Too bad he got saved by his silly wife. Not his wife.
> Now he's got to go on being alive
> Like all the rest of us here who survive.
> I stay alive so Frank may as well.
> He won't go to heaven and he's already in hell.
> Poor Frank was never very cheerful —

She stops, stuck for a rhyme.

BECKY. Except when he goes to the pub and then he's beerful.

They laugh.

ANGELA. Those pills must have made him feel sick
And wish he'd never followed his prick.

They laugh.

BECKY. That's quite good.

Silence.

ANGELA. Becky, why do you like me? I don't want you to like me.

Silence.

BECKY. Poor Frank. Imagine.

Scene Twenty

VAL *and* SHONA.

VAL. Shona. I hoped I'd see you.

SHONA. I've been to the shop for nan.

VAL. What did you get?

SHONA. Sliced loaf, pound of sausages, butterscotch Instant
Whip, and a Marathon for me and Deb, I'm going to cut it in
half. The warts have gone off my hands because nan said get
some meat and she got some meat yesterday and it was liver
and it wasn't cooked yet but she cooked it for tea but I didn't
like it but I liked the bacon. She cut off a bit and rubbed it on
my warts, Deb said Eugh. Then me and Deb buried it in the
garden near where nan's dog's buried. There was one here and
one here and another one and some more. I watched 'Top of
the Pops' last night and I saw Madness. Deb likes them best
but I don't.

VAL. What do you like?

SHONA. I don't like Bucks Fizz because Mandy does. She's not
my friend because I took the blue felt tip for doing eskimos
and Miss said use the wax ones but I have to have felt tips so I
got it and Mandy says she won't choose me when it's sides.

VAL. She'll probably have forgotten by tomorrow.

SHONA. Nan says you mustn't cut your toenails on Sunday or
the devil gets you.

VAL. It's just a joke.

SHONA. My toenails don't need cutting because nan cut them
already. What hangs on a tree and it's brown?

VAL. What?

SHONA. Des O'Conker. What's yellow and got red spots?

VAL. The sun with measles.

SHONA. Knock knock.

VAL. Who's there?

SHONA. A man without a hat on.

VAL. What?

SHONA. Why did the mouse run up the clock?

VAL. Why?

SHONA. To see what time it is.

VAL. Shona, when you grow up I hope you're happy.

SHONA. I'm going to be an eskimo. Mandy can't because she can't make an igloo. She can come on my sledge. Nan said to be quick.

VAL. Why does an elephant paint its toenails red?

SHONA. Footprints in the butter.

VAL. No, that's how you know it's been in the fridge.

SHONA. Why then?

VAL. So it can hide in a cherry tree.

SHONA. Deb knows that one. Nan doesn't.

SHONA goes.

Scene Twenty-One

VAL *and* FRANK.

VAL. I've got it all worked out.

VAL pulls up her shirt.

VAL. Look. I marked the place with a biro. That's where the knife has to go in. I can't do it to myself.

FRANK. I can't even kill a dog.

VAL. I've been feeling happy all day because I decided.

FRANK. You marked the place with a biro.

VAL. I know it's funny but I want it to work.

FRANK. It's ridiculous.

VAL. Just say you love me and put the knife in and hold me till it's over.

VAL gives FRANK the knife.

FRANK. We don't have to do this.

Silence.

VAL. Say you love me.

FRANK. You know that.

VAL. But say it.

FRANK. I nearly did it. I nearly killed you.

He puts the knife down.

VAL. Do it. Do it.

FRANK. How can I?

VAL. Just do it.

Silence.

FRANK. Aren't you cold? I'm shivering. Let's have a fire and some tea. Eh, Val?

FRANK *picks up an axe and is about to go out.*

Remember —

VAL. What?

FRANK. Early on. It wasn't going to be like this.

Silence.

Why do you — ?

VAL. What?

FRANK. All right then. All right.

He kills her with the axe.

He puts her body in the wardrobe.

He sits on the floor with his back against the wardrobe door.

She comes in through the door on the other side of the stage.

VAL. It's dark. I can see through you. No, you're better now.

FRANK. Does it go on?

VAL. There's so much happening. There's all those people and I know about them. There's a girl who died. I saw you put me in the wardrobe, I was up by the ceiling, I watched. I could have gone but I wanted to stay with you and I found myself coming back in.

There's so many of them all at once. He drowned in the river carrying his torch and they saw the light shining up through the water.

There's the girl again, a long time ago when they believed in boggarts.

The boy died of measles in the first war.

The girl, I'll try and tell you about her and keep the others out. A lot of children died that winter and she's still white and weak though it's nearly time to wake the spring — stand at the door at dawn and when you see a green mist rise from the fields you throw out bread and salt, and that gets the boggarts to make everything grow again. She's getting whiter and sillier and she wants the spring. She says maybe the green mist will make her strong. So every day they're waiting for the green mist.

I can't keep them out. Her baby died starving. She died starving. Who?

She says if the green mist don't come tomorrow she can't wait. 'If I could see spring again I wouldn't ask to live longer than one of the cowslips at the gate.' The mother says, 'Hush, the boggarts'll hear you.'

Next day, the green mist. It's sweet, can you smell it? Her mother carries her to the door. She throws out bread and salt. The earth is awake.

Every day she's stronger, the cowslips are budding, she's running everywhere. She's so strange and beautiful they can hardly look. Is that all? A boy talks to her at the gate. He picks a cowslip without much noticing. 'Did you pick that?'

She's a wrinkled white dead thing like the cowslip.

There's so many, I can't keep them out. They're not all dead. There's someone crying in her sleep. It's Becky.

FRANK. I can hear her.

VAL. She's having a nightmare. She's running downstairs away from Angela. She's out on the road but she can't run fast enough. She's running on her hands and feet to go faster, she's swimming up the road, she's trying to fly but she can't get up because Angela's after her, and she gets to school and sits down at her desk. But the teacher's Angela. She comes nearer. But she knows how to wake herself up, she's done it before, she doesn't run away, she must hurl herself at Angela — jump! jump! and she's falling — but it's wrong, instead of waking up in bed she's falling into another dream and she's here.

BECKY *is there.*

BECKY. I want to wake up.

VAL. It's my fault.

BECKY. I want to wake up. Angela beats me. She shuts me in the dark. She put a cigarette on my arm. She's here.

ANGELA *is there.*

ANGELA. Becky, do you feel it? I don't, not yet. There's a pain somewhere. I can see so far and nothing's coming. I stand in a field and I'm not there. I have to make something happen. I can hurt you, can't I? You feel it, don't you? Let me burn you. I have to hurt you worse. I think I can feel something. It's my own pain. I must be here if it hurts.

BECKY. You can't, I won't, I'm not playing. You're not here.

ANGELA *goes.*

NELL *crosses on stilts.*

NELL. I was walking out on the fen. The sun spoke to me. It said, 'Turn back, turn back.' I said, 'I won't turn back for you or anyone.'

NELL *goes.*

SHIRLEY *is ironing the field.*

SHIRLEY. My grandmother told me her grandmother said when times were bad they'd mutilate the cattle. Go out in the night and cut a sheep's throat or hamstring a horse or stab a cow with a fork. They didn't take the sheep, they didn't want the meat. She stabbed a lamb. She slashed a foal. 'What for?' I said. They felt quieter after that. I cried for the hurt animals. I'd forgotten that. I'd forgotten what it was like to be unhappy. I don't want to.

FRANK. I've killed the only person I love.

VAL. It's what I wanted.

FRANK. You should have wanted something different.

The BOY *who scares crows is there.*

BOY. Jarvis, Jarvis, come and make my coffin.

VAL. My mother wanted to be a singer. That's why she'd never sing.

MAY is there. She sings.

Girls' Song

Methuen Modern Plays

include work by

Jean Anouilh
John Arden
Margaretta D'Arcy
Peter Barnes
Brendan Behan
Edward Bond
Bertolt Brecht
Howard Brenton
Simon Burke
Jim Cartwright
Caryl Churchill
Noël Coward
Sarah Daniels
Nick Dear
Shelagh Delaney
David Edgar
Dario Fo
Michael Frayn
John Guare
Peter Handke
Declan Hughes
Terry Johnson
Kaufman & Hart
Barrie Keeffe

Larry Kramer
Stephen Lowe
Doug Lucie
John McGrath
David Mamet
Arthur Miller
Mtwa, Ngema & Simon
Tom Murphy
Peter Nichols
Joe Orton
Louise Page
Luigi Pirandello
Stephen Poliakoff
Franca Rame
David Rudkin
Willy Russell
Jean-Paul Sartre
Sam Shepard
Wole Soyinka
C. P. Taylor
Theatre Workshop
Sue Townsend
Timberlake Wertenbaker
Victoria Wood

Methuen World Classics

Aeschylus (two volumes)
Jean Anouilh
John Arden
Arden & D'Arcy
Aristophanes (two volumes)
Aristophanes & Menander
Peter Barnes (two volumes)
Brendan Behan
Aphra Behn
Edward Bond (four volumes)
Bertolt Brecht
  (three volumes)
Howard Brenton
  (two volumes)
Büchner
Bulgakov
Calderón
Anton Chekhov
Caryl Churchill
  (two volumes)
Noël Coward (five volumes)
Sarah Daniels
Eduardo De Filippo
David Edgar
  (three volumes)
Euripides (three volumes)
Dario Fo (two volumes)
Michael Frayn
  (two volumes)
Max Frisch
Gorky
Harley Granville Barker
  (two volumes)

Henrik Ibsen (six volumes)
Lorca (three volumes)
David Mamet
Marivaux
Mustapha Matura
David Mercer
  (two volumes)
Arthur Miller
  (four volumes)
Anthony Minghella
Molière
Tom Murphy (three volumes)
Peter Nichols
  (two volumes)
Clifford Odets
Joe Orton
Louise Page
A. W. Pinero
Luigi Pirandello
Stephen Poliakoff
Terence Rattigan
Ntozake Shange
Sophocles (two volumes)
Wole Soyinka
David Storey
August Strindberg
  (three volumes)
J. M. Synge
Ramón del Valle-Inclán
Frank Wedekind
Oscar Wilde